The 6 Literacy Levers

The 6 Literacy Levers

Creating a Community of Readers

Brad Gustafson

ConnectEDD Publishing
Chicago, Illinois

This publication is available at discount pricing when purchased in quantity for educational purposes, promotions, or fundraisers. For inquiries and details, contact the publisher at:
info@connecteddpublishing.com

Published by ConnectEDD Publishing LLC
Chicago, IL
www.connecteddpublishing.com

Cover Design: Kheila Dunkerly

The fable within this book is a work of fiction. Names, characters, locales, and incidents are either from the author's imagination or are used fictitiously. Any resemblance to actual persons, business establishments, or schools is entirely coincidental.

The 6 Literacy Levers/ Brad Gustafson. —1st ed.
Paperback ISBN 978-1-7361996-7-1

Praise for *The 6 Literacy Levers*

Rarely am I able to pick up a book and immediately find what Brad Gustafson refers to as "Reading Flow." When I started reading *The 6 Literacy Levers*, I was immediately enticed by the number of ideas, supports, and reflective opportunities embedded throughout the book. Brad finds creative ways to balance his experiences and knowledge with a humbleness that allows ALL readers to feel as if becoming a literacy leader is within their reach!

—Matthew Arend | Educational Consultant

The 6 Literacy Levers is by far one of the best literacy books I have read in a long time. The book provides simple, concrete, step-by-step guidance on how to ignite the literacy community in your school building. Once I started *The 6 Literacy Levers*, I couldn't put it down. I self-reflected on my literacy practices the entire time I was reading the book. The levers provide a clear understanding and framework for implementation. This book has the capability of transforming schools across our nation.

—Dana Boyd | Teacher of the Year (TX) and National Distinguished Principal

Dr. Brad Gustafson provides educators with practical insights, applicable tools, and a powerful "why" for leading this work forward in *The 6 Literacy Levers*. Readers will walk away with a clearinghouse of thought-provoking questions and tangible takeaways that can be applied in their classrooms and schools.

—Jessica Cabeen | National Distinguished Principal, NAESP Middle-Level Fellow, Principal, and Author

Regardless of your role in education, Brad has provided us with key areas that will support literacy in our schools. Packed with strategies and valuable exercises, *The 6 Literacy Levers* will challenge your thinking while providing strategies to take this much-needed work to the next level. Gather your people, engage in authentic discussions, and jump-start your "reading flow" with a book that will elevate literacy leadership.

—Dr. Lynmara Colón | Director, Author

Hooked right from the start! *The 6 Literacy Levers* pulls you in close and tugs at your heartstrings. The book will take you on a journey filled with reflection and exploration while illuminating six levers to become a literacy leader. This is a book I wish I had years ago during my first year as an elementary principal. Brad Gustafson makes you feel seen, heard, and inspired when it comes to understanding the challenges we face every day as leaders of literacy while providing hope and strategies to help move forward in a positive way. *The 6 Literacy Levers* is a book all educators need.

—Dr. Rachael George | NAESP Fellow, Author, and Speaker

Brad Gustafson extends an invitation to literacy leadership to each of us in his latest book, *The 6 Literacy Levers*. He combines a rich and easy narrative with research and literacy-building tools that inspire the reader toward concrete action. You'll appreciate the valuable resources strategically embedded throughout the book. Develop a culture fueled by a desire to read for pleasure as you dive into *The 6 Literacy Levers*.

—Pam Gildersleeve-Hernandez | Experienced Superintendent
    and Non-Profit CEO

I love the messages to all literacy leaders and their responsibility to assist students with cracking the reading code. As a literacy leader, it was great to read that we *can* break the code. Code breaking can't be done without instruction in vocabulary, context, and communication patterns. I can't wait to build my literacy legacy using the six levers shared in this book. You and your school community will grow from every lever shared by Brad. A great resource!

—Tracy Hilliard | National Distinguished Principal

Brad absolutely nailed it with *The 6 Literacy Levers*! Infused with a sense of urgency and grounded in research, Brad provides honest and reflective stories, memorable analogies for tools, and templates for implementation. *The 6 Literacy Levers* is loaded with takeaways I can't wait to implement in my school right now!

    —Andy Jacks | National Distinguished Principal and Author

Regardless of the role you serve in your school, *The 6 Literacy Levers* will inspire you to lead literacy with enthusiasm and confidence. Gustafson masterfully weaves an empowering message that will take you wherever you are in your literacy leadership journey and guide you forward. With a mix of robust research, relatable stories, specific ideas you can implement now, and activities to guide you and your team, this book is full of practical insights. Each chapter gave me something to take away, and I am more empowered to lead in my current role than I've ever been thanks to Brad's impactful message.

    —Sarah Johnson | Library Media Specialist, Leadership Coach,
       and Author

The 6 Literacy Levers is a great resource for teachers, administrators, and other literacy leaders. It will help us make a significant difference in the reading lives (and thus directly improve the academic success) of our students. It's brimming with ideas, strategies, and tools to build a community of engaged readers. I'm confident this book can help us reach every student, no matter their struggles, attitudes, or beliefs, and support them in becoming avid readers.

    —Ben Kort | Teacher-Librarian and District Library TOSA

We understand how critical literacy is for opening doors and allowing each individual to reach their full potential. As such, developing the skills and enthusiasm for literacy, not just doing well on a test, should be foundational in each and every school. *The 6 Literacy Levers* will guide you to create the conditions that empower young people to thrive as readers and writers. This book should be mandatory for all educators, not just ELA teachers, to read and put into practice.

—Katie Martin | Author of *Evolving Education* and *Learner-Centered Innovation* and Chief Impact Officer at Learner-Centered Collaborative

For decades, improving student literacy has been at the heart of many educational debates from federal policy circles to local faculty meetings. Rates have remained stagnant, and many educators have grown weary of the reading war mud-slinging. Finally, a new resource has arrived to help fundamentally alter the conversation. In *The 6 Literacy Levers: Creating a Community of Readers*, award-winning principal Brad Gustafson shares an evidence-based roadmap to create dynamic reading experiences for each learner while providing practical ideas to help guide your personal journey forward. Whether you're a principal leading the conversation at a school level, or a teacher working alongside students each day, this book is a foundational resource for all who serve our nation's children.

—Thomas C. Murray | Director of Innovation, Future Ready Schools® Washington, D.C. and Best-selling Author of *Personal & Authentic*

There are few people I've met who are as passionate about literacy as Brad Gustafson. This book is straight from his heart and filled with incredible takeaways. I know this is a book I'll not only continually be referring back to, but one I'll be buying multiple copies of to share with friends.

—Todd Nesloney | Educator, Author, Speaker, and Director of Culture & Strategic Leadership for TEPSA

The 6 Literacy Levers has the potential to change the lives of the readers you serve. I hope you'll purchase this book and read it with all the educators in your building. I can't wait to share it with my colleagues!

—Colby Sharp | 5th Grade Teacher and Co-founder of the Nerdy Book Club

The 6 Literacy Levers is a must-read for any educator who wants to take their literacy game to the next level for their students and staff. Dr. Gustafson not only equips the reader with best practices but also gives day-to-day examples that will have a direct impact on students tomorrow. *"Literacy leadership doesn't start with an initiative. It starts with an authentic invitation"* is a message that needs to be shared in every teachers' lounge.

> —Curtis Slater | Co-Founder of TILL360 Consulting and
> National Distinguished Principal

Brad Gustafson draws on his years of experience as a school leader, literacy advocate, and reader to guide you in not only WHAT to do, but also an actual HOW and WHY. The evidence-based research he provides as context for each of the levers will help leaders everywhere redefine a subject that should not just be taught, but enjoyed and loved. His passion for students to have access to authentic, quality literature as well as the life-changing opportunities a book can provide is sure to get you fired up. Easy to read, easy to implement, this book should make its way into the hands of teachers and leaders everywhere.

> —Amber Teamann | Director of Technology & Innovation
> and Author

The 6 Literacy Levers provides tools and strategies for school teams and district leaders. Educators will be able to reflect on their priorities and sense of urgency for developing lifelong readers. This book will serve as a guide for school teams who are seeking to transform schoolwide reading practices and literacy experiences!

> —Dr. Steven Weber | Associate Superintendent for Teaching
> and Learning

Dedication

Whether you're leading literacy from the classroom, board room, or beyond: This one's for you...because we owe it to them!

Table of Contents

Introduction

The Story Starts Here

Imagine this: You're meeting with a parent in distress. Their eyes flash with intensity and regret. And you know you're not the only one seeing it. The co-workers who have joined you for the meeting shift in their seats, too.

The most uncomfortable part of the meeting might be that the parent hasn't raised their voice. Rather, they are spitting facts. Their child is struggling with reading and has been for years. A different approach might have yielded different results. The school, your school, hasn't tried anything different. Their child only has one year before they move on; less than nine months to do whatever it takes to turn their reading identity around. For good.

As you listen to the parent's pointed questions, a dangerous thought flits through your mind. You casually look in the direction of one of your co-workers. She's the literacy expert on staff. You're hoping she can provide the answers. Her attention intensifies on the parent. You reluctantly refocus as well.

You start to wonder what it would be like to have a pause button on your chair. Or a time machine. Anything that would allow you to find solutions to the situation unfolding in front of you. And then an uncomfortable quiet fills the room.

You look towards the parent. *Can they read minds, too?!* If they could, they'd know you don't have the answers. You're not even sure you know what questions to ask. But at this moment, your commitment and care could not be more genuine.

You cling to this commitment with every fiber of your being, sitting up a little straighter in your chair. Instinctively, you nod in agreement with the parent's imperfect pleas. You're willing to own your part of this situation, which is a pretty big part. Because you're a leader. And leaders lead—by learning.

Maybe it's not a time machine or escape button you need after all. Maybe you just need a little help finding a better handle on literacy. Because your leadership matters, and you want to leverage it to help all students succeed. And right now, they're not.

> *"Somebody is looking to you to lead right now."*
> *~Richard DuFour & Robert Marzano (2011)*

From Story to Practice

Each of us has probably experienced something in our careers that stopped us in our tracks. Maybe it was a meeting with a supervisor that still stings. It might have been seeing lackluster test scores published in the local newspaper next to your school's name. Or perhaps it's something even more personal like seeing a student struggle with reading, despite years of intervention and support.

Leadership is uncomfortable because it's personal. The success of our school, team, and students informs how we identify as a leader. Their success is our success, which means when they fail, so do we. This is probably why leadership can feel overwhelming at times, too.

At the same time, the number of priorities competing for our attention is staggering. Regardless of whether we're leading from the classroom or board room, or somewhere in between, at any given time we are juggling, supporting, and influencing many things. Suffice it to say, I understand.

As an elementary principal, I do my best to navigate all the "things" competing for my attention. And as an author and speaker, I get to engage with leaders around the world who are struggling with some of the same things we are wrestling with. Hard things. Exciting things. Embarrassing things. Seemingly impossible things. But also hope-filled things, empowering, and world-changing things. All these things require strong leadership.

Growing readers is also one of these "things." In many ways, it is *the* thing that should (and does) influence all other things. That's because students who are successful readers have the capacity to be more successful in nearly every other academic area (Irvin, 2010). And highly effective leaders make reading a top priority so that students can be successful (Daniels & Steres, 2011). Unfortunately, it's not easy. If it were, we would all be seeing dramatically different results.

For decades, roughly sixty percent of 4th and 8th graders have not been proficient in reading, and forty percent of high school graduates in the United States haven't had the literacy skills prospective employers were seeking (Houck & Novak, 2016). Worse yet, the longer students are in school, the less they enjoy reading (Wigfield, Gladstone & Turic; 2016).

While it might be easier to admit we have a reading problem in this country, I want us to consider the possibility that we also have a leadership opportunity. And just like the story that started this chapter, if we're willing to own our part of the problem, we can be part of the solution.

Leaders play a critical role in creating the conditions that ensure both the *skill* and *joy* of reading are revered. When our colleagues observe a lack of commitment towards the literacy program coming from leadership, the discretionary energy they're willing to invest decreases dramatically (Edmonds; 2011 & NASSP; 2005). Schools with successful literacy programs show evidence of strong principal leadership that leverages all aspects of school operations to champion readers (Booth & Rowsell; 2007).

We know reading is important. Teaching kids to read is a ubiquitous goal in schools. However, we also must strive to teach kids who WANT to read long after all their reading-related assignments are completed. And also in between these assignments. In part, because the joy of reading is strongly linked to learning (Sullivan & Brown; 2015).

Reading for pleasure is more important to cognitive development in adolescence than parents' level of education (Jacobson, 2017; Sullivan & Brown; 2015). Increasing students' motivation to read also improves reading comprehension and the frequency in which students choose to read (Becker, McElvany & Kortenbruck, 2010; Kusdemir & Bulut; 2018). The motivation to read is an important mile marker on the pathway to improving student achievement and long-term success.

> Every student has the right to learn how to read. Every student deserves a literacy-rich environment in which reading is championed by the leaders in their school.

Every student has the right to learn how to read. Every student deserves a literacy-rich environment in which reading is championed by the leaders in their school. This book provides people at every level of leadership the tools and culture-building strategies needed to help all students fall in love with reading.

About this Book

- This book is for any educator who wants to grow as a *literacy leader*.
- This book will empower teams to *initiate conversations* that will take the work deeper.
- This book explores *six literacy levers* that will help you push the field forward while creating more enriching reading experiences for the readers you serve.

♦ This book will equip you with actionable ideas and the research needed to *activate change*.

This book was *not* written by a reading-policy expert. But it was written by a school leader who understands many of the complex challenges confronting educators. I've sat with families who were needing help while being unable to provide the answers they deserved. I've been frustrated trying to do work that matters without having enough time or support to do it. And I've struggled to simply show up during an unrelenting pandemic.

But I haven't done any of these things from *your* classroom, school, or office. I don't know *your* students or community like you do. My vantage point is limited. The solutions readers need are bigger than anything I could hope to write. Which is why the six literacy levers are incomplete without *your* background, expertise, and discernment.

Similarly, the strengths and stories readers carry with them must be present in the decisions made on their behalf. Each of the literacy levers requires you to apply your own insights and personal touch. As I previously mentioned, I am underequipped to tell you how to respond to the needs of the readers you serve. One thing I can share is how the incredible team I get to work with has risen to this opportunity.

We started asking different questions about reading. We worked from a place of passion and used curiosity to confront the literacy practices doing damage to readers. We shared our reading lives, and in turn, saw students share more of theirs. And we refused to stay stuck—even when the places we were stuck in seemed rather comfortable.

We're still learning, but the change we're creating is undeniable. And we're not alone. Literacy leaders across the country are leveraging their strengths to activate change and create a culture of literacy. This book will highlight some of their stories as well as my own. In this way, you'll see how educators from different states and levels are seeing results.

Many of these results are accompanied with ideas to support implementation in your sphere of influence. Sometimes the examples will reflect the strengths and readiness level of your community. Other times, you'll be stretched to make connections to your role—or the level you're serving in. It's important to remember this work—and the results we seek—requires an active commitment to learning. No matter the content area, domain, or level you're leading, you can create a community of readers.

Chapter Summaries

Introduction: The Story Starts Here
You've heard the urgent pleas of a parent who is concerned about their child's reading, but how will you respond? This introduction highlights the importance of reading leadership.

Chapter 1: The Compass
Taking steps to grow as a literacy leader means building on the existing strengths that already fuel you and your team, while developing new ones. This chapter will help you and your team create a literacy compass that reflects your strengths and vision while being responsive to the needs of the readers you serve.

Chapter 2: The Invitation
Literacy leadership doesn't start with an initiative. It starts with an authentic invitation. This chapter will help you accept that invitation, find your reading flow, and invite others into the work as well.

Chapter 3: The Walking Stick
Asking the right questions is almost always better than sharing the right answers. Like a faithful walking stick, this chapter will help you lean on questions. When carried consistently, these questions will take conversations deeper as you push the field forward.

Chapter 4: The Utility Knife
One of the most versatile tools literacy leaders have at their disposal is the "booktalk." The simple act of sharing a book recommendation

creates connection, increases motivation, and transforms culture. This chapter unpacks the power and potential of *booktalks* in practical, how-to terms.

Chapter 5: The Catapult
Vision and urgency alone will not propel your school's reading culture forward. This chapter will help you harness the power of relationships and connection as you co-create and strengthen your school's reading community.

Chapter 6: The Collage
The final lever might be the most powerful force in literacy leadership. This chapter will empower you to own your influence and activate change. You'll be presented with tools and resource options to help you implement what you're learning in a manner that makes the most sense to you and your team.

Special Features

The book you're reading was designed to empower leaders in class-rooms, libraries, offices, and every space in between. It includes ideas and strategies to support educators at every level because leadership isn't reserved solely for those who hold a specific job title.

On a similar note, I'm convinced the path forward must be a path for everyone. There isn't a single reader in your school who doesn't deserve to be seen, supported, and included. This book includes levers and cautionary advice to help you respond to practices that could damage, diminish, or exclude any of the readers you serve. Just as I would never want my own children to come home from school in worse condition than how I sent them (physically or emotionally), literacy leaders have a responsibility to serve on behalf of all readers. Here are some additional features found within the book:

Story-Based Narratives: Every chapter starts with an immersive 2nd-person narrative that puts you in the center of the action. These stories were designed to create and nourish existing connections between you and the relational work in which you are invested.

> There isn't a single reader in your school who doesn't deserve to be seen, supported, and included.

Action-Oriented Questions: Reflective questions reinforce the theme of each chapter. You'll find additional questions to help you push the field forward near the end of every chapter.

Practical Levers: Each chapter focuses on a specific tool or strategy you can leverage in your leadership role. The levers are introduced in the opening story and are accompanied by ideas to help you put them into action.

Dictionary-Style Graphics: This highlighted vocabulary will help you add clarity to your goals and hit the ground running with a common language. The clear and compelling definitions emphasize the topics that matter most.

Activities to Support Growth and Schoolwide Implementation: Part personal-growth tool and part schoolwide implementation guide, the activities in each chapter provide a step-by-step pathway to creating a culture of reading.

On-Demand Support: I hope you'll use your favorite social media platform to connect with me and other literacy leaders using the hashtag for this book (#LiteracyLever). If you're interested in a hands-on workshop, culture-building keynote, booktalk training, or discount on bulk purchases, go to my website (BradGustafson.com) to initiate an inquiry.

CHAPTER 1

The Compass

Imagine this: You step inside your favorite café and are met by the familiar chorus of coffee grinders. You've always appreciated the way this place makes you feel. Focused and inspired.

Your feet glide over a well-worn compass inlaid into the hardwood floor. Before you're even in line, you're greeted by Dayo's ear-to-ear smile. He's the college-aged barista who has been working here the longest. Seeing him behind the counter is a sign that good things are in store. Not just for the work you're planning to tackle, but for your coffee, too.

After ordering, you make your way to your favorite table. You pause to look at the collection of polaroid pictures hanging on the wall. You recognize a few of the faces, but even the unfamiliar smiles somehow put you at ease.

With a heavy sigh, you spread out your research. It feels as though you've read some of this stuff hundreds of times. *Aside from classroom instruction, nothing influences learning in a school more than leadership* (Wahlstrom et al., 2010).

You reach for the steaming cup in front of you and wince. The coffee is great, but everything else on your plate is tricky. You're being asked to lead increasingly complex work without enough time or support to do it. At least not well.

Most times, you put your best foot forward and try to manage. But sometimes it's a struggle just to put out the fire burning hottest. Being forced to choose which of the school's priorities you have enough bandwidth to actively engage with doesn't feel like leadership to you. It doesn't seem...CLANK!

Your table is jarred, and a small pool of coffee appears around the base of your cup. A woman and young boy are now reading at the table next to yours. She's absorbed in a novel and the young boy is clumsily scooping marshmallows out of his hot cocoa while flipping through the pages in a book. You recognize it instantly because it was one of the first books you read growing up. *Who could forget that ravenous caterpillar?*

In the opposite corner of the café, you spot Dayo standing next to a customer with a towel under his arm. The customer has dark, wavy hair with purple highlights. The two of them are laughing at something the young woman is reading. Dayo is pointing at the cover and shaking his head enthusiastically. *That's Dayo for you.*

Seeing the young woman and Dayo having the joy-filled exchange over a book is smelling salt to your soul. You scan the coffee shop again. The different ways people are connecting stirs something inside you. And it makes you want to change the way people experience reading in your school.

You spend the next couple of hours looking at leadership articles through a different lens. Literacy, relationships, and connection. These are the things that have driven you as an educator for years. Maybe not the literacy part, but you decide this, too, can change.

You know literacy, relationships, and connection are inherently linked. They cannot be seen as something separate from the day-to-day work being done in classrooms and schools. And the research in front of you confirms this. *When leaders approach initiatives as separate silos their impact dramatically decreases* (Wallace Foundation, 2013).

You look up and notice the young boy and his mom are gone. A few marshmallows are scattered underneath their table. And then you see it.

The caterpillar book is on the floor next to the compass. The large wooden needle inlaid into the floor appears to be pointing directly to the book. You start to think about that sticky story and all it represents. With a humble confidence, your attention shifts back to the compass. Now, you're the one who's smiling.

- What research and leadership axioms are currently guiding your work?
- How would you describe your "true north" when it comes to literacy?

"It's not about perfection, it's about direction."
~Jan Richardson, Ph. D. | Literacy Expert

From Story to Practice

A compass has very little to do with perfection. No path is perfect. The compass is about direction. It's your purpose and vision for readers. And the obstacles you're willing to navigate to help them come together as a community.

It's easier to think about who you want to be as a reading leader in moments of inspiration. But the day-to-day demands of the work make it much more difficult to transform vision into action. A literacy compass will empower you to be more purposeful in your leadership.

Leaders who have the greatest influence in the world tend to understand the importance of purpose (Sinek, 2009). Movements are fueled by it. People are compelled by it. Identifying your purpose inspires

Figure 1.1: **The Compass Defined**

action, but it also creates a sense of belonging (Michels & Murphy, 2021).

Purpose allows people to make connections between their strengths and their mission. It provides direction while empowering us to tap into our strengths along the journey. Going on a journey without leveraging any of your strengths would be ill-advised. The key is carrying a compass that provides direction but also reflects your strengths.

Activating Your Strengths

Anytime you're using a compass, you want it to be true. True for you and true for the readers you serve. But here's the thing. Nobody knows your school like you do. Simply put, I can't tell you what's true about much of the work you do. One thing I can tell you is that readers benefit when *everyone* in a school and community brings their strengths to the work. Developing a better understanding of who you are and the strengths others see in you is also important. This will help you stay true to yourself while you're providing leadership to others.

The first step in activating your strengths is to stop devaluing yourself. Minimizing your strengths and overlooking your skills is one of the top barriers to success identified by leaders (McCullough, 2020). The following activities will help you see your strengths and apply them to a literacy compass you create.

1. This foundational work of literacy leadership starts with you. I've symbolically placed the starting point for this activity on the bottom of figure 1.2. Start by listing a few of the leadership strengths, attributes, or skills you see in yourself in the section labeled "Self."
2. Next to each of the strengths or attributes you just jotted down, add an example or description. For example, if one of the strengths you listed was "Communication," you might add where you see your best work with communication being done.
3. Sometimes we miss seeing the things in ourselves that others value most. Connect with a trusted co-worker or colleague and ask them if they'd be willing to talk through a few strengths they see in you. Write down what you hear in the section labeled "Co-Worker."
4. Another important aspect of knowing yourself involves understanding how friends or family members see you apart from your professional work. They often have insights into your strengths and identity that even your closest co-workers might not notice. Connect with a friend or family member and ask them what strengths they see in you when you are at your best

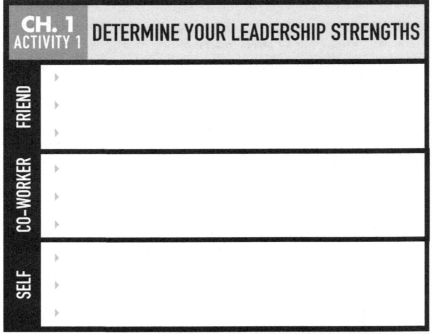

FROM "THE 6 LITERACY LEVERS" BY BRAD GUSTAFSON (2021)

Figure 1.2: **Determine Your Leadership Strengths (Activity)**

outside of work. Write down what you hear in the section labeled, "Friend."

5. Highlight or underline the strengths that you'd like to see represented in your literacy compass. Be purposeful in tapping into your strengths.

6. Take time to revisit all these strengths regularly.

The readers you serve are counting on you to move forward with purpose and as your authentic self—with all your strengths. You want these strengths to be so sticky that it's impossible to envision moving forward without them...like the marshmallow fingerprints on that caterpillar book.

Finding Your Way

Many leaders have a favorite quote or mantra. Perhaps it's a line from a book that resonates or a research finding you reference frequently. On your best days, these quotes can inspire your actions and inform your decision-making. On most other days, they take a back burner to the myriad of other things competing for your attention.

The next activity will help you move some of the research and thinking that inspires you most to the front burner where it's accessible in your everyday leadership. Along with your strengths, this thinking will help you create a literacy compass you can carry with confidence.

1. Write down a few of your favorite leadership quotes and core beliefs. Don't worry about whether they relate directly to literacy yet. I wrote down a few quotes connected to purpose and vision that have guided my thinking recently:

"Clear is kind. Unclear is unkind."
Brené Brown

"Where there is no vision, the people perish."
Proverbs 29:18

"Leadership is the capacity to transfer vision into reality."
~Warren Bennis

"I don't care about what you expect; I care about what you model."
~Tom Murray

"For there is always light, if only we're
brave enough to see it.
If only we're brave enough to be it."

~Amanda Gorman

2. Reread the leadership quotes and/or core beliefs you just wrote down. Choose one that really resonates and write it down in the middle of the compass (see figure 1.3). I created an example on the left-hand side of the figure but ignore the additional text by the plus and minus signs for now.

3. Now, it's time to think about your quote in terms of literacy leadership. Think about what it might look like if you were to

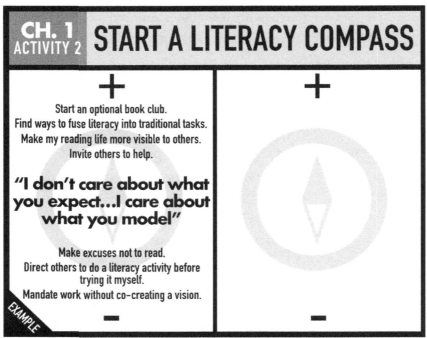

FROM "THE 6 LITERACY LEVERS" BY BRAD GUSTAFSON (2021)

Figure 1.3: **Create a Literacy Leadership Compass (Activity)**

apply your quote to literacy in a meaningful manner. List several actions or ideas above the quote near the plus sign. Challenge yourself to write down actions or ideas that also reflect your strengths.

4. It can be fun to think about what your literacy leadership might look like when things are moving in the right direction. However, when things go south it's usually because we allowed the complexities of the work (e.g., office politics, failure to prioritize, not maintaining relationships) to compromise the mission. Write down a few of the actions or approaches you want to avoid near the minus sign directly underneath your quote.

5. Creating your literacy leadership compass is more than a theoretical endeavor. Put your beliefs into action by reviewing the list of ideas you jotted down near the plus sign. Choose one of the ideas and implement it.

You've taken risks and tried new things before. Use an implementation process you've had success with in the past to move forward on your idea. I also want to emphasize the importance of starting small. This is a theme you'll see carried forward through many of the implementation challenges in the book. Never underestimate where a series of small and purposeful steps will take you.

Building the Bridge

People often talk about practicing strengths-based leadership, but sometimes it comes across as more of a sound bite than an actionable leadership strategy. I want to share an example of how activating your strengths and putting your literacy leadership compass to work can look.

I'm passionate about amplifying student voice. I also have a lot of experience helping school leaders use technology to better connect with their communities. These are both strengths of mine. So much so that I wrote a book, *Renegade Leadership: Creating Innovative Schools for Digital-Age Students*, focusing on these areas.

A big part of that book is about connecting your knowledge and strengths to the places students need you to lead. After all, it doesn't do any good to stay stuck in your strengths if your strengths don't connect to what readers actually need.

As difficult as this is to admit, there was a time in my leadership when I was stuck in my strengths. I had allowed my passion for technology leadership to overshadow what readers needed me to be doing on their behalf. This could turn out to be a long list, but here are a few examples:

+ I was largely unaware of the current books students were reading.
+ I definitely couldn't hang with other educators when it came to talking about newer picture books.
+ And when it came to Y.A. authors, I struggled to recognize anyone's name unless they wrote *Hatchet* or *Charlotte's Web.*

Instead of fixating on what I couldn't do yet, or how I felt like a fake, I leaned into a couple of my strengths and passions. It was the only way I knew how to try and get unstuck.

Before I share more about how this worked, I want to mention that a significant portion of this book will highlight the ideas, inspiration, and research of other literacy leaders. However, for this first chapter I share more about how I stumbled through things initially. I thought it might be helpful to hear how some of the small steps I took alongside more established literacy leaders in our school helped me grow. This next story is an example of how this worked for me.

I started by using my experience with technology and video-production to create a series of short booktalk videos to share with staff. Creating the videos motivated me to read more. The more booktalk videos I created, the more comfortable I grew with talking about books, which led to me seeking out some of the avid readers on staff to converse about reading.

At first, it felt awkward and fake for me to even try to enter into these conversations. Or share booktalks with others. I tried to tuck these feelings of inadequacy aside and leaned further into my purpose and who I knew I wanted to be for the readers in our school. Eventually, the way I was using social media started to evolve. This led to my co-hosting #30SecondBookTalk with Jennifer LaGarde. What started out as a technology-based collaboration (because that's where my strengths were) evolved into a connected literacy project involving literacy leaders from around the world.

My passion for technology was eventually eclipsed by a genuine love of reading and a commitment to help all readers experience success. It wasn't long before I was infusing literacy into most of my work as a principal.

The annual new-teacher introduction videos we created also started showcasing book recommendations from staff and students. We even designed a digital booktalk backdrop and used the backdrop in some of our videos (see figure 1.3). It was a blast!

Fast-forward to today, and it's impossible to take more than a few steps in a classroom or hallway without being reminded of the fact that you're amongst a community of readers.

This story demonstrates how building a bridge from your strengths to who readers need you to be as a literacy leader can work regardless of where you're leading from right now. I don't think there's a perfect starting place or single path for this work. But there is you, your team, and everything that's worked for you in the past. There's also what's needed moving forward, and somewhere in between is a bridge.

Debbie Mercer is the Dean of the Kansas State University College of Education. Her research on school leadership has helped inform how institutions of higher education are preparing the next generation of leaders. Mercer (2016) has framed change leadership as, "Moving

Figure 1.3: **Literacy-Infused New Staff Introduction Video**

from what worked in the past, to what is needed in the future" (p. 9). Effective leaders know how to bridge an organization's past successes with the work that's required to remain relevant and responsive in the future.

I'll be the first to admit, bridging your past successes with literacy leadership isn't always easy. Starting with your strengths doesn't guarantee you'll always feel strong.

The Benefits of Imposter Syndrome

There are still times when I'm talking about books or doing read alouds in classrooms when it feels a little forced. It happens less now than it used to, but I've noticed the feeling pops up when I start to compare myself to others.

If you've ever doubted yourself or felt somebody else was more equipped to lead, you're not alone. Imposter syndrome is another one of the top barriers leaders encounter (McCullough, 2020). As you start to grow into the literacy leader you want to become, I want to offer a counter narrative to the negative pep talks you may be tempted to provide yourself.

There are actually benefits to feeling unequipped, fraudulent, or as though you're not prepared to be in a certain leadership arena. First off, if you're feeling like somebody else is more qualified to do the work you're being called to do, you can use that to fuel your commitment to learning. It's also an opportunity to be transparent about your journey. When you make mistakes moving forward, because we all do, your honesty and humility can help others who may be struggling with new learning or afraid to start.

Imposter syndrome is evidence of an invaluable leadership trait: humility. I'd be worried if you felt you were overly qualified to lead literacy. This reminds me of a cognitive bias that's the opposite of imposter syndrome. The Dunning-Kruger effect describes a person who thinks they're highly skilled, but in reality, has an extremely low level of competence (Kruger & Dunning, 1999). I guess you could say that another benefit to feeling like an imposter is that you know you're not suffering from the Dunning-Kruger effect.

While these benefits may sound good, my best advice is to resist the temptation to compare yourself to other literacy leaders. Try to look at their expertise as an asset or resource instead of something that makes you feel inferior. Viewing the knowledgeable and confident colleagues surrounding you as a system of support is the mindset required to optimize growth and overcome imposter syndrome (Shepherd & Taylor, 2019).

I came across a quote recently that might be a good contender for the center of your compass—especially if you're just starting this journey:

> *"Being willing to do what you are not qualified to do is sometimes what qualifies you."*
>
> *~Bill Johnson*

21

Evolving as a leader...changing culture...pushing the field forward. This work is a journey. The compass can help you take purposeful steps forward. It can also help you recognize when a practice or policy feels like it's not serving all readers. Or when you and your team might be unknowingly headed in the wrong direction.

A Word of Caution

Just because a school has a strong vision and compass in place doesn't mean missteps won't happen. Rerouting is a natural part of any journey, similar to when you're driving with a Global Positioning System (G.P.S.) or phone navigation on and miss a turn.

During my first year as principal in my current school district, I had a lot of meetings at different buildings throughout the district and I had no idea where I was going. Ever. I remember one particular day when I typed in the destination for a meeting into my phone but got lost anyway. There was one point where my G.P.S. was telling me to take an endless series of left turns around a median in our high school parking lot. It was so frustrating. But here's the thing. I recognized I needed rerouting. The key was me having an awareness that something wasn't right—which was rather obvious since I was circling the median in a parking lot. There will be times in your literacy leadership journey that you or your colleagues are spinning. Only nobody will be holding up a large-blinking sign that says, "Rerouting." Pay attention to your instincts in these moments. Look at the words and core beliefs on your compass. You might be one of only a few people in an entire school who is in a position to notice a practice or conversation that needs rerouting.

Obviously, the negative consequences that can result from not noticing a potentially harmful educational practice is far greater than circling a median or being late to a meeting. When we miss opportunities to reroute practices, we run the risk of doing long-term damage to students' relationship with reading. The harm that can happen is very real, and it usually happens when our compasses don't champion all readers—or when we fail to notice when something requires rerouting. Perhaps you've encountered some of these instances:

+ When *some* students are regularly empowered with choice in their reading and *others* are not.
+ When *some* students consistently see themselves represented in books in beautiful, powerful, and authentic ways and *others* do not.
+ When *some* students get to enjoy daily independent reading time with no strings attached and *others* do not.
+ When *some* students are placed in environments where reading for pleasure is seen as a right and *others* are subjected to an endless barrage of forced written responses every time they read.
+ When *some* students receive explicit decoding instruction and *others* are not given the tools they need to unlock text.

Each of these things is problematic, but it takes somebody to notice, reroute, and change culture. For all kids. Whether you're leading from the classroom, main office, or beyond, the time to lead using a compass that serves all readers is now. That is literacy leadership.

Your Literacy Leadership

I want to be clear about what I mean when I use the term "literacy leadership" (see figure 1.4). I see literacy leadership as something that's active and serves all readers. It is also something that doesn't exist in a vacuum. In other words, I see value in connecting your literacy leadership to the work other literacy leaders are doing in your classroom, school, and beyond. I wouldn't advise closing the door to your office or classroom and trying to practice literacy leadership alone. There's so much we can learn and do together.

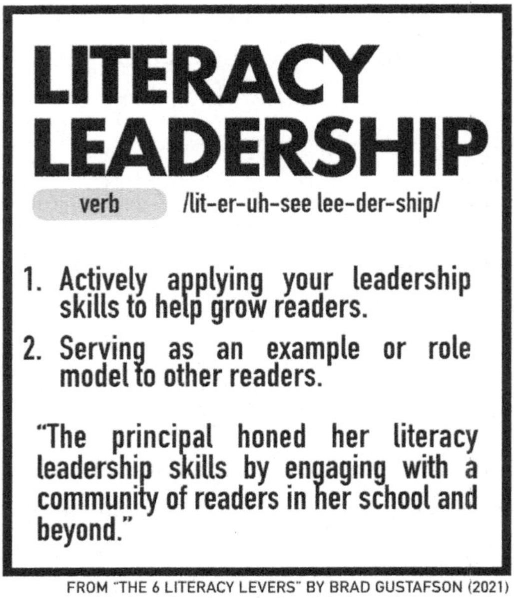

LITERACY LEADERSHIP

verb   /lit-er-uh-see lee-der-ship/

1. Actively applying your leadership skills to help grow readers.
2. Serving as an example or role model to other readers.

"The principal honed her literacy leadership skills by engaging with a community of readers in her school and beyond."

FROM "THE 6 LITERACY LEVERS" BY BRAD GUSTAFSON (2021)

Figure 1.4: **Literacy Leadership Defined**

Since literacy leadership is an active verb, I want to share a few ideas you and your team might consider trying as you're working together to live out your purpose. Of course, you can activate your strengths and compass to build the bridge in other ways, too. I just want to be sure you have some support to answer the questions, "*So now what?*" and "*What might this look like?*"

Ideas You Can Implement

I'm always surprised at how taking the smallest of steps can create momentum and lead to unexpected growth. I also love how the ideas of others inspire me to take additional steps forward on the bridge. An example of this type of inspiration comes from an incredible middle-school principal in New York. Dr. LaQuita Outlaw makes it a point to travel the hallways in her school with a book in hand. From the thrills of morning duty to the shrills of the playground, staff and students will often see Dr. Outlaw carrying a book. She refers to this practice as the *Traveling Book* (see figure 1.5).

Dr. Outlaw sees the *Traveling Book* practice as a relationship builder and better conversation starter than talking about the weather. It also helps her model how to carve out reading time in between other important commitments. It's not unusual for her to take a moment in between talking with students and staff to read a few pages.

You can *tell* students how important reading is. You can also *tell* them how much you love reading. But if we're doing more *telling* than *showing* there's going to be a disconnect. We're doing it wrong if we tell

Figure 1.5: **Dr. Outlaw's *Traveling Book***

students how important reading is, but they've never seen us carrying a book we're reading for pleasure.

Several literacy leaders in our school display signs outside their classrooms showing what they are reading. Similar to Dr. Outlaw's approach, this helps students connect on different levels. A few years ago, I followed suit and started displaying my monthly read alouds in my office window (see figure 1.6).

> We're doing it wrong if we tell students how important reading is, but they've never seen us carrying a book we're reading for pleasure.

The simple act of sharing more of my reading life has led to me being invited into more book-related conversations in our school and community. I've also noticed that the practice of literacy leaders sharing their reading lives using simple signage has evolved into something we're all doing. And I never saw the tipping point coming.

The cultural shift became clear several years ago at a district data retreat. Some of the leaders on staff suggested we formally adopt the

Figure 1.6: **Monthly Read-Aloud Sign**

practice as something we would all do. At the time, I was less bold and suggested we keep the practice as optional. However, a robust discussion helped me understand that this was something that could be a difference-maker for readers. After all staff engaged in the sharing, it didn't take long for students to join in (see figure 1.7). The conversations we get to have with readers as they're updating their "Currently Reading" signs are something I cherish.

Reimagining Routines

Another way our school has tried to follow the compass is by looking at our routines and traditions through a literacy lens. This activity will help you reimagine some of the routines your school has in place to move further into your purpose as a literacy leader.

Figure 1.7: **Currently Reading Hallway Signs**

Think about a specific routine or tradition in your school. Any routine, tradition, leadership practice, or event will do. Whether it's school assemblies, open house, budgeting, conferences, report cards, parent communication, staff meetings, or school-improvement planning.

1. In the box labeled "Before," write down the name of a routine on the line (see figure 1.8).
2. List some of the basic steps or parts of the routine in the space below the line. To give you an idea of how this works, I'll use "School Pictures" as an example. In thinking about the routine of school pictures in our elementary school, several steps come to mind:

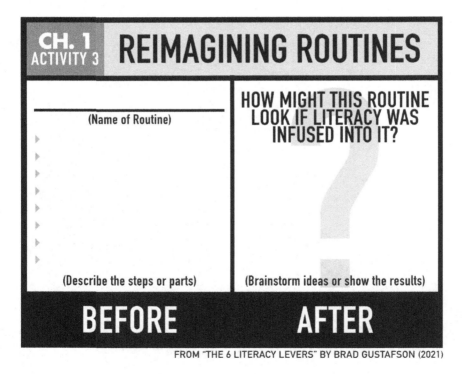

FROM "THE 6 LITERACY LEVERS" BY BRAD GUSTAFSON (2021)

Figure 1.8: **Reimagining Routines (Activity)**

- Select date and sign contract with the vendor
- Communicate with staff, families, and volunteers
- Send home order forms and create a schedule
- Support the set-up process and volunteers
- Staff and students have their pictures taken
- Support the clean-up process and thank volunteers
- Repeat the process on retake day
- Send picture orders home
- Create and display large staff composite photo
- Ensure yearbook team has access to pictures

3. Now that you've listed some of the steps involved with the routine you selected, read the reflective question in the box labeled "After." *How might this routine look if literacy was infused into it?*

4. Use the space in the "After" box to brainstorm and write down different ideas. You don't need to come up with a grandiose change or completely transform an event that was working well. Consider some of the small ways you might infuse literacy into any of the steps.

5. Choose an idea to implement. Work with your team to reimagine the routine.

In case you were wondering, our team reimagined school pictures by infusing reading into the staff pictures we had taken (see figure 1.9). We invited staff to bring a favorite book to picture day. We also had a cart full of classic stories and some newer releases in case a staff member forgot to bring a book. Hearing the conversations staff had about the books they selected over the course of the entire school day was priceless.

The result of reimagining school routines and leadership practices are often long lasting. In the case of school pictures, we created a giant staff composite and hung it in the main hallway (see figure 1.10). Seeing students search for the teachers and books they love as they walk by each day is pretty awesome.

Figure 1.9: **Reimagining School Pictures**

School pictures are something our school typically does towards the beginning of the year. Another example of a routine we reimagined takes place towards the end of the school year.

For years, we were invited by our PTA and yearbook advisors to write a special message to students. I always tried to encourage students while wishing them a good summer. However, my yearbook messages have evolved over the years just as my growth as a literacy leader has. For the past several years, we've included a few book recommendations in yearbook messages to students (see figure 1.11).

When we started the practice, I figured a few families might read the message and that even fewer would take the time to check out the books I recommended. I definitely didn't expect anyone would ever circle back to discuss the books with me. However, that's exactly what has happened.

Figure 1.10: **Reimagining School Pictures - Staff Composite Photo**

It makes sense that our efforts to connect readers to books they might want to read make a difference. Not only in terms of creating culture, but also in terms of achievement. One study (Sullivan & Brown, 2015) involving more than 3,500 people in Britain found that reading for pleasure during childhood plays a more significant role in cognitive development during adolescence than a parent's level of education. Our efforts to lead in a manner that is inclusive and motivating to all readers can also lead to very unexpected results.

One summer, I received a call from a parent who had discovered my yearbook message in her child's yearbook. She went on to tell me that she had gone to college with Dusti Bowling, an author of one of the books I had recommended. We chatted for a while and I remember hanging up and thinking how cool it was to have that time and connection.

Figure 1.11: **Yearbooks Messages with Book Recommendations**

You can imagine my surprise when a few days later, Dustin Bowling and I connected (thanks to the help of the parent)! At one point in our conversation, I asked Dusti if she'd be willing to share a video message with our school and reveal some fun facts or something surprising about her book, *Insignificant Events in the Life of a Cactus*. She obliged and we were able to share that video message with students. Talk about an unexpected surprise on multiple levels!

Questions to Push the Field Forward

+ How might we create more joy-filled reading experiences?
+ How will you ensure your vision reflects the strengths and assets of your entire school community?

Leverage Your Literacy Leadership Schoolwide

Creating systems that support and inspire all readers requires visionary leadership and collaboration. But it also requires us to see readers as whole and complete people.

> *"They are readers, but they are also artists, athletes, writers, gamers, and musicians. For me, this is what wild reading is: readers who incorporate reading into their personal identities to the degree that it weaves into their lives along with everything else that interests them."* (Miller & Kelley, 2014, p. 3)

This type of vision and understanding will sharpen your compass and help you create an enriched reading environment, one in which students choose to read when they don't have to—like the joy-filled reading experiences happening in the café from the story at the beginning of this chapter.

Engage with the ideas in this book as a team to help grow a culture of literacy schoolwide. Research your current vision for readers (see figure 1.12). Challenge yourself to partner with others to co-create a shared compass. The compass you and your team create can take any shape. Some schools create a vision for literacy that's maintained as a living document and referenced often. Other schools work together to create a list of reading rights: things all students can expect as they interact with books and each other. I've even seen schools that have created massive word walls using Scrabble-style letter tiles to display their core values.

Create a compass or other symbol that is meaningful to you and your school community. Talk about your compass and commitments often. Then, live them out with unrelenting fervor. If you want literacy to become part of your school's culture, you need to create a compass that everyone can see themselves reflected in.

CH. 1
ACTIVITY 4 **CREATE A COMPASS**

SCHOOLWIDE IMPLEMENTATION CHALLENGE

1. Start small – research what your school's vision for literacy is and explore other related work

2. Collaborate with your team to create or update your vision for literacy

3. Look for a meaningful way to display your shared beliefs...then live them out in all you do

"MAMA SAYS...BEING STRONG MEANS MOVING FORWARD. 'TINY STEPS ARE FINE,' SHE SAYS, 'AS LONG AS THEY TAKE YOU IN THE RIGHT DIRECTION.'"

BE STRONG BY PAT ZIETLOW MILLER

FROM "THE 6 LITERACY LEVERS" BY BRAD GUSTAFSON (2021)

Figure 1.12: **Schoolwide Implementation Challenge**

CHAPTER 2

The Invitation

Imagine this: You're not sure why, but you decide to pick up the sticky, marshmallowy book that was left behind. There's a bookmark barely peeking out from underneath the front cover. You check both sides hoping to find the young boy's name or a clue that might help you return the book to his family. Your jaw drops.

The boy's name is nowhere to be found. But yours is. And the thing you thought was a bookmark is actually an invitation. You scan the café for hidden cameras. Then, you turn your skepticism in Dayo's direction. "This is absurd," you say as you exchange glances between the invitation and Dayo, who takes a few steps away from a table he's cleaning.

Dayo leans in to take a closer look. His head tilts ever-so-slightly as his eyebrows scrunch up. It's a look you seldom see on him. As he looks over your shoulder, he mumbles your name followed by the rest of the words printed on the invitation:

You're invited to have dinner with your favorite author, literacy expert, or reading champion. Dinner is at 7:00 p.m. Check your phone for details. Who will you choose?

"Who will you choose..." As Dayo rereads the last sentence you're already digging in your pocket. Nobody else has access to your phone, so you sense the ruse coming to an end. There will be no new details on your device. And there will be no dinner. As your thumb slides across the screen, a small curse word escapes your lips. You know you don't have dinner plans—at least you didn't before coming in for coffee. But the calendar invite you're staring at says otherwise. "What the...?"

Dayo clears his throat and nods in the direction of a table with a toddler. The toddler starts babbling something that sounds similar to the colorful word you just spoke into the universe. Your eyebrows and shoulders shoot up as if to say there was no better word to describe this turn of events. A subtle eye roll and small smirk from Dayo suggests he sees things differently.

You continue to scroll through your phone, and it appears you've already accepted the invitation. Before you're able to delete the calendar item, Dayo asks, "Who will you be inviting for dinner?" Hearing him ask the question makes this ridiculousness start to feel real.

You try to muster up an answer before responding but aren't sure what to say. Dayo's genuine smile gives you the confidence to respond. There *is* somebody in the reading world who has inspired you for quite some time.

- If you could meet a favorite author or reading champion for dinner, who would it be and why?
- What are some questions you'd like to ask if you had the chance to meet with a favorite author or reading champion?
- Describe a time you were invited into something special?

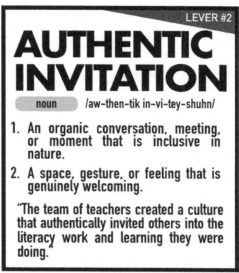

FROM "THE 6 LITERACY LEVERS" BY BRAD GUSTAFSON (2021)

Figure 2.1: **Authentic Invitation Defined**

"Sometimes the greatest gift you can give another person is to simply include them."

From Story to Practice

Never underestimate the power of an authentic invitation. Many people spend the better part of their lives wanting to be included (Gillies, 2017). To experience the kind of belonging that not only recognizes their strengths, but also meets their messiness and missteps with grace. These kinds of invitations are hard to come by, but when you're involved in one, you feel it in your soul.

Unfortunately, the invitations deployed by school leaders can sometimes feel different. I'm not trying to pile on principals, but a mass email soliciting help with lunchroom duty or attempting to fill a vacant committee position is not the kind of invitation I'm talking about. Non-coercive invitations reflect the needs of the person receiving the invitation and not just the needs of a committee, department, or school (Staloch, 2002). This doesn't mean those of us serving in formal leadership roles can't share authentic invitations. It just means we have to work that much harder to build trust and serve others.

> Authentic invitations are often organic. They are personal and purposeful. Authentic invitations have more to do with feeling and less to do with formality.

Authentic invitations are often organic. They are personal and purposeful. Authentic invitations have more to do with feeling and less to do with formality. This is why some of the most authentic invitations come from people who don't have formal leadership titles.

Most people appreciate it when a colleague requests their input or invites them to collaborate on meaningful work. This doesn't mean they're always able to say "yes." But it does feel good to be included, respected, and valued.

I don't know about you, but sometimes it's easier for me to start thinking about a concept in a different application or setting. This helps me see past some of the mental hurdles my mind would ordinarily trip over if I tried to jump right into applying that same concept to literacy leadership.

A Different Kind of Invitation

I still remember the time a few teacher-leaders in our school started a new event called "SpheroExo." In a nutshell, the event was the elementary equivalent of a robotics battle arena.

The rules were simple. Students were placed on a team and issued a Sphero robot, push-pins, and a balloon. Their goal was to design and engineer a 3D-printed exoskeleton that protected their balloon, but also included offensive capabilities so they could pop other teams' balloons.

Each year, the teacher-leaders who conceptualized the SpheroExo event invited me to create my own SpheroExo. My job was to take on the winning team's SpheroExo in an ultimate showdown. And I took the job very seriously.

One year, I engineered a motorized helicopter blade using supplies from our school's mobile makerspace carts (see figure 2.2). I even tipped the propeller with push-pins. It looked incredibly cool when the motor was turned on, but there was just one problem.

It was way too heavy. The additional battery and scaffolding needed to support the rotor created so much friction against our gym floor that my robot had a difficult time dragging everything around. Consequently, the team of students I competed against in the championship this particular year used their nimble design to destroy my balloon—and my pride.

As principal, I loved seeing students work together to design their SpheroExos. I loved seeing staff take risks to champion collaborative learning experiences. I even got goosebumps seeing families packed inside our gym to cheer on their children. But the thing I loved most was being included and seeing the strong sense of belonging students also experienced. The invitation matters.

Your literacy leadership might not have anything to do with 3D printing, robots, or balloons, but it probably will involve people serving in pockets of excellence who are committed to meaningful change. The authentic invitations exchanged by these small and mighty groups can be a culture-building force.

Small and Mighty

Ashley Martin, Teri Webb, and Gary Moser know a thing or two about authentic invitations. And starting small. They are 4th-grade teachers

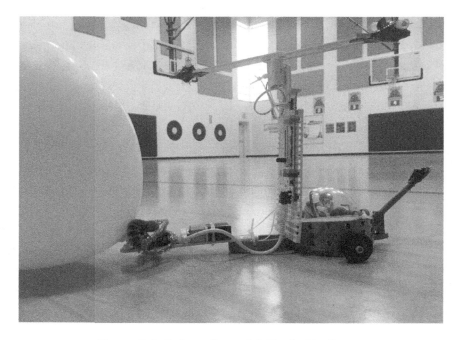

Figure 2.2: **SpheroExo with Push-Pin Rotor**

and a literacy leadership force at Springside Elementary in the Alpine School District. With the help of their school's media specialist, Jennifer Miller, they've helped move their school's culture of reading forward in big ways.

I heard about the inspiring work they were doing from their principal, Gary Gibb, while working with the Utah Association of Elementary School Principals. A few weeks after talking with Gary, I was able to connect with his 4th-grade team to learn more about their work together.

It turns out, each of them had been leading literacy within the walls of their classroom for several years. (In Gary's Moser's case, it had been for more than thirty years!) It took a series of authentic invitations to bring the team together around a shared compass.

For the Springside Elementary team, these authentic invitations involved the organic sharing of research on reading motivation and making reading its own reward. It also included collaborating on a literacy fellowship from Utah Valley University (UVU) that helped fuel and inform their work together. The two-year fellowship included monthly professional development opportunities and research provided by the UVU team. Each month, the team would work together to incorporate what they were learning into their classrooms.

This grew into a collective commitment to cultivating the curiosity of readers through thematic teaching. Some of the invitations also involved honest dialogue about practices that might be damaging the reading identities of some students.

All these invitations—the sharing of research, conversations, collaboration, and honest dialogue—may have seemed like small things at the time. But they have led to mighty results. Results ranging from shifts in thinking to systemic changes impacting the trajectory of students' reading lives.

Gary Moser shared a story about a student who was really fighting reading. The student hated school and wasn't shy about letting his teachers know it. Seeing his classmates reading books that were several grade-levels above the books he was struggling with only exacerbated the problem.

Over the course of the school year, Mr. Moser invited the student into a relationship. By seeing the student's strengths. Listening. And sometimes just by being there. During this time, Mr. Moser recognized the student did not like being told what to do or what to read. Mr. Moser leaned into what he was learning about reading enjoyment while continuing to teach the student fundamental skills needed to read.

Progress was slow and the student continued to struggle—and not just with reading. Sometimes it seemed as though nothing was making a difference. At least that's how it appeared.

Years later, Mr. Moser ran into him outside of school and received some surprising feedback from the young man. He said, "Mr. Moser, you gave me hope." Let that sink in.

The authentic invitations being shared by the Springside Elementary team were making a difference on multiple levels. Here are a few additional results the team has also achieved together:

- They have reignited their own passion for teaching reading.
- They stopped using a reading program that was damaging the reading identities of students.
- They are part of a growing community of teachers who believe in the power and joy of reading.
- They co-create schoolwide literacy experiences that bring books and beloved characters to life.
- They increased their individual and collective efficacy as reading teachers.
- Their ability to cite and apply relevant research to literacy instruction has increased.
- They lead presentations at reading conferences.
- They created a display celebrating readers and the goals they set for themselves.
- They're helping to change mindsets and making reading the reward.

Authenticity

Each of the examples above is a story in itself. The team and I took time to talk through many of them. I'm not able to convey all the inspiring work they're doing, but I did ask the team what they felt was the key to the results they were achieving. Without hesitation, they shared that they are readers first. There's an authenticity to the work they're trying to do, which makes the invitations they share with their students and colleagues authentic. Before the team invites anyone into anything, they model what it means to be a reader.

Readers know when you're genuinely into a book, book character, or content area. But they also know when you're preaching something you don't practice. There's a profound difference between a teacher who says, "*You* should read this…" and a teacher who says, "Can *I* read that when you're done?"

Because the Springside Elementary team is on the journey and authentically walking the walk, they're more equipped to help others with their journey. They are able to talk about what a genuine reading life looks, sounds, and feels like because they're living authentic reading lives. This includes the times they're ravenously reading a book, but it also includes the times they may struggle to start reading.

Working through different levels of reading motivation themselves puts them in a better position to invite students into authentic reading behaviors. For example, instead of giving a student grief about not finishing a book, the Springside team actually teaches students how and when to consider abandoning a book. Authenticity enhances impact.

The Thing about Literacy Leaders

At the beginning of this chapter, you received an invitation to have dinner with an author, literacy expert, or reading champion. Of course, I'm curious about whom you might like to connect with. I've given this scenario some serious thought and I have more than a few names in mind. Regardless of who you or I might choose to meet, I can guarantee you one thing: They would be a reader. The person you pick would have a genuine relationship with books.

Pernille Ripp is a middle-school educator, author, and expert in literacy and technology integration. She's also the creator of the *Global Read Aloud* and one of the most credible voices in literacy I know. Pernille recently shared a quote on social media that stated, "*If you see no value in the books in your library, why should students? If you say you have no time to read, why would students?"* (Ripp, 2021).

While Pernille's question may have been rhetorical, the answer that pops into my head is, *"They shouldn't. And they wouldn't."*

Of course, there will always be some students (and staff) who will make reading a priority despite our example, but they shouldn't have to. We should never risk being a non-example for any reader. Readers deserve to have countless reading role models in their lives.

Seth Godin, a world-renowned author and entrepreneur who was recently inducted into the Marketing Hall of Fame, says it like this: "People like us do things like _____" (Godin, 2020). You and I might say something like this instead: *Leaders like us read.*

You can be passionate about other things, too, but you must have a personal relationship with books. It's this relationship that elevates your thinking when it comes to curriculum decisions, scheduling, and countless other things.

Unfortunately, many school leaders who share the responsibility of being a reading champion don't have this type of relationship with reading yet. This makes them more susceptible to settling for surface-level literacy advocacy and less equipped to examine the things that steal precious time away from readers during the school day (Havran, 2019). Fortunately, there is a place literacy leaders can go to take their relationship with reading deeper.

Reading Flow

Growing up, getting an invitation to attend a friend's birthday party was one of the coolest things that would happen. One of the first things I'd look for on the invitations was where the party was being held. Understanding how reading flow works is like being able to provide people directions to the party.

People want to know where they're going. Location matters. One of the most important places we can invite others is the reading flow zone. The reading flow zone (see figure 2.3) is the literacy equivalent to 'flow' that was first introduced by Mihaly Csikszentmihalyi in 1990.

> Understanding how reading flow works is like being able to provide people directions to the party.

Finding your reading flow zone requires an awareness of what your reading life looks, sounds, and feels like when things are going well. Because here's the thing: your reading life won't always flow. You'll encounter speed bumps and distractions that pull you away from reading. Pretending these impediments don't exist is not an effective literacy leadership strategy. Neither is waiting until you feel a strong motivation to read.

READING FLOW ZONE

noun   /ree-ding floh zohn/

1. The feeling of being completely engrossed in a text or reading-related experience.
2. A mental state marked by an increased motivation to read.

"The student teacher believed that in order for readers to find their flow zones, their reading identities needed to be nurtured and protected."

FROM "THE 6 LITERACY LEVERS" BY BRAD GUSTAFSON (2021)

Figure 2.3: **Reading Flow Zone Defined**

Many people mistakenly think they should wait until they feel a strong desire to read before they actually start reading. Here's a dirty little literacy secret: waiting for the perfectly motivating book to fall in your lap while you're in the middle of a distraction-free environment doesn't work. If you are waiting for your reading motivation to be stronger than any other force in your life, you will be waiting a long time.

The readers you serve are counting on you to figure this out. Every cause needs a catalyst, and the literacy leader's catalyst is reading. Here is a list of things readers say to help move into the flow zone (see figure 2.4). These are the directions to the party I mentioned earlier—the reading party!

I am going to talk through a few of the things readers say when they're moving into their flow zone. Trying only one or two of the

FINDING READING FLOW
SIX THINGS READERS SAY TO GET IN THE ZONE

1. I CHOOSE WHAT I'M READING OR IT WAS RECOMMENDED BY SOMEBODY I RESPECT
2. I ACTUALLY START READING
3. I ENJOY WHAT I STARTED READING OR CHOOSE SOMETHING ELSE TO READ
4. I EMBED READING INTO (OR IN BETWEEN) THE OTHER PRIORITIES I HAVE
5. I TALK ABOUT WHAT I'M READING
6. I CARRY WHAT I'M READING WITH ME

FROM "THE 6 LITERACY LEVERS" BY BRAD GUSTAFSON (2021)

Figure 2.4: **Finding Reading Flow**

steps probably won't produce life-changing results. However, working through all the steps in a progression just might help you find the place you've been looking for.

Of course, the factors that help me find my reading flow zone will be different than yours. Consider this list as a starting place. You'll want to adapt and change it until the steps better support your reading identity and preferences. With that said, here's a quick overview of the list.

Choosing what you read is important. There have been times I've received books from a supervisor that I previously had my eye on. However, when these books became required reading my motivation to read changed. Invitations and choice are inherently more motivating than assignments.

Choice alone doesn't guarantee you will find the reading flow zone. You actually have to start reading—and then enjoy what you're reading. This is why it's so important to model how to abandon books that are sucking the motivation out of your reading life. Forcing yourself to read the wrong book for you isn't fair. To anyone.

After you've chosen a book and confirmed that it's enjoyable, it's important to make time to read. Easier said than done, right? If you're looking for large chunks of uninterrupted time, you might be looking for a while. I'd suggest stealing minutes before appointments, in the car while waiting for family or friends, before bed, etc. This is a great way to capture extra time to read; just be careful you don't take it too far. I remember one evening, my wife and I were on a double date with friends we hang out with on a regular basis. I decided to bring a book I was into just in case there was a break in the action. At one point, we were in between rounds in a card game we enjoy, and everyone busted out their phones to check their social media feeds. I figured this was my chance to pull my novel from my jacket and started reading. They gave me a hard time about this, but to this day I don't see why my reading was less acceptable than theirs.

Either way, the story illustrates the gravitational pull books can have when you find the reading flow zone (which I was clearly in). I should probably emphasize, my desire to read is not always this high. Reading is a relationship. And just like the relationships we maintain with friends and family members, there are feelings, decisions, and seasons of life that can pull us away.

Find Your Reading Flow Zone

Understanding the conditions that help and hinder your reading flow zone matters. For starters, it enhances your ability to provide leadership that will help, not hinder, the reading lives of students. You might think this ability would come naturally to all leaders, but data suggest otherwise.

The longer students are in school, the less they enjoy reading (Wigfield, Gladstone & Turic; 2016). To compound the problem, the motivation to read doesn't necessarily return when students graduate. Albeit a smaller sample size, Penny Kittle asked her university students about their reading habits. Half of them reported never reading books and 20 percent indicated they rarely read (Kittle, 2020).

This activity will change the math! By understanding the factors that motivate you to read, you'll be more effective with the readers you serve.

1. Reflect on the conditions that motivate you to read. Try to think about the people, places, times, genres, and other environmental considerations that positively correlate to your reading.
2. Write down a few things that positively influence your reading motivation on the right-hand side of the continuum (see figure 2.5). I call the right side of the continuum the *flow zone* because it represents some of the things that spark your interest in reading.

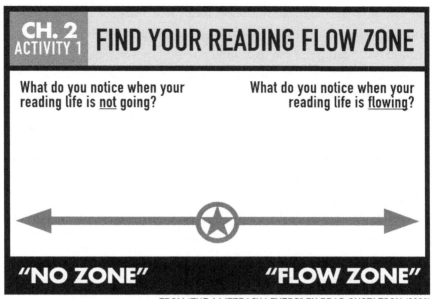

FROM "THE 6 LITERACY LEVERS" BY BRAD GUSTAFSON (2021)

Figure 2.5: **Find Your Reading Flow Zone (Activity)**

3. Next, try reflecting on the things you see as demotivators to reading. Think about what you notice when you're not reading.

4. Write down a few things that negatively impact your reading motivation on the left-hand side of the continuum. I call this side the *no zone* because if we stay in this space too long, we will get little to no reading done.

5. Try to be more intentional with how you structure your daily routines and decisions. See if you can make small changes that start to create the conditions that draw you into the flow zone. For example, if you find yourself more motivated to read after talking to a specific teacher who loves literacy, try adding more frequent visits with that person into your weekly schedule.

I look at the star on the continuum and imagine it sliding back and forth depending on my mood, environment, and the distractions around me. Seeing the star as a slider should give you a pretty good idea of just how fluid (and elusive) reading flow can feel at times.

I still remember the first few months of the COVID-19 pandemic. My family had been self-quarantining to protect a medically fragile relative. My motivation to read was at an all-time low even though I had more time at home than ever before. (It probably didn't help that the complexity and demands at work were at an all-time high.) No matter what I tried, I couldn't seem to get out of the "no zone."

I was eventually able to move closer to the middle of the continuum, a place where I could at least manage turning a few pages a day. Getting there took a long time. My point is, don't feel bad if your reading life isn't flowing yet. Or if your life circumstances make it difficult to fathom reading for fun. It happens.

A Word of Caution

There will be times when you feel as though something is hindering students' reading lives, but your colleagues see value in that very same thing. The topic of reading rewards seems to boomerang back year after year, so I want to go there for a moment.

Instead of outright condemning reading rewards, I'm going to invite you to go back and review the conditions you identified as being part of your reading flow zone. These are the things you listed on the right side of your continuum that spark your interest in reading or make it more enjoyable.

I love pizza as much as the next person, but I'm guessing you did not identify pizza or free ice-cream coupons as the primary motivating forces in your reading life. That's because people tend to be motivated by deeper needs like the desire to direct their own lives, to create, and to learn new things (Pink, 2009). I would also add the feeling of connection to the list.

When we want to use a reading-related reward, our school uses things like free-book coupons, bookmarks designed by readers, and extra reading time. Sometimes the extra reading time involves glow sticks, dress-up days, and flashlight reading. We find these reading-related experiences create an additional level of connection while still being closely linked to reading.

Ideas You Can Implement

As a principal, I've found four strategies that have helped me jump-start my reading flow during the school day (see figure 2.6). This has been key because they keep me connected to reading when time and

FROM "THE 6 LITERACY LEVERS" BY BRAD GUSTAFSON (2021)

Figure 2.6: **Four Ways to Jump-start Your Reading Flow**

energy are in short supply after school. It's no coincidence they all involve authentic invitations in some way.

Start a literacy-themed project with students: Gabe Hackett is the principal at Little Mountain Elementary in Monticello, Minnesota. He's invited students to participate in a booktalk video project with an engaging DJ theme. If readers love listening to music or aspire to be YouTubers outside of school, why not help them reach their goals in school?!

One year, our school was lucky enough to partner with Gabe on the project. Students from each of our schools recorded their book-talk videos separately, and then Gabe and I edited them together and shared the combined videos with each of our school communities. It was kind of like dueling BookTalk DJs. A newspaper in Gabe's neck of the woods captured a behind-the-scenes look at his booktalk DJs in action (see figure 2.7).

Figure 2.7: **BookTalk DJs in Action**

The BookTalk DJ concept helped increase students' confidence with sharing books, and their motivation to participate was off the charts. You know you've arrived when talking about books is so cool students are begging to do it!

To get the project going on our side of things, I would share information about becoming a BookTalk DJ with an entire grade-level. After that, teachers sent permission slips home. Once the permission slips started coming back, I worked with small groups in the office. We'd have a working lunch, converse about books, and then bust out the DJ gear.

The approach helped me build relationships with students, but it also created protected time in my schedule to actually eat lunch. Creating the videos on a weekly basis provided me with additional reading accountability. Working with students on the literacy-themed project helped to jumpstart my own motivation to read on a more regular basis.

Prioritize reading in your budget and schedule: Schools with a strong culture of reading make reading a top priority (Daniels & Steres, 2011). I was chatting with a colleague recently who helped me see how her school's budgeting process was enhanced by reading data and an invitation to students to be part of the process.

Dr. Kari Wehrmann is an elementary principal and former ELA teacher in Minnesota. Her school's Parent Teacher Association (PTA) tries to do one larger fundraiser each year to support special projects. As part of the process, the PTA chooses one project to fund that becomes the focal point of the fundraiser. This builds momentum by providing her school community with a clear sense of where money will go.

Dr. Wehrmann and her team decided their main project would be rejuvenating classroom libraries to support students' independent reading. In preparation, she asked teachers to purge their classroom libraries of books that were damaged, old, or rarely chosen. Teachers who were new on staff weeded through the books they inherited, and more experienced teachers sorted through books they had accumulated from thrift stores, garage sales, and with publishing points over the years. The weeding process alone revealed dramatic inequities between the quality and quantity of books in different classrooms.

Around the same time, the district where Dr. Wehrmann and I both work was modernizing collections. This process produced data that showed a need for more current non-fiction, and high-quality books that were representative of a diverse student body. Dr. Wehrmann's team was able to use this same data to help inform the purchases they planned to make.

After the PTA fundraiser, Dr. Wehrmann and her school's PTA invested the fundraising dollars to rejuvenate classroom libraries and support the school's media center. Every classroom teacher received a portion of the money to spend. Dr. Wehrmann asked teachers to spend one-third of their money on filling their classroom library's specific gaps (e.g., more books for emerging readers), one-third on books students would help select, and the final third on books that students could see themselves in.

At the time, over 40 percent of her school's student population was Asian-American, and primarily the Indian culture. The literature in classrooms was not serving as *windows, mirrors,* or *sliding glass doors* for many students (Bishop, 1990). As Rudine Sims Bishop has said, books that serve as windows allow readers to view another person's experience. Books that serve as mirrors reflect our own culture and story. And books that serve as sliding glass doors allow students to step into a story and transform their perspective—allowing them to bring a renewed perspective back to the real world.

To find current topics and authors that reflected Indian culture, media specialists across the district curated a list of high quality, engaging, elementary-appropriate books from various publishing companies. Dr. Wehrmann's staff curated an electronic list of suggested books, guidelines for the purchases, and spreadsheets detailing who was ordering what on a Google site, so grade level teams could coordinate purchases and glean ideas from their colleagues.

As the books arrived, positive ripples were felt by their entire reading community. For instance, one girl held a book up reverently, saying, "I get to read a book about a girl who looks just like me. I've never seen me before." Students experienced an additional level of ownership because they helped select so many of the books. One teacher gift-wrapped all the books for her classroom and videotaped the class as they enthusiastically opened the presents. Dr. Wehrmann shared that video in a weekly newsletter to her school's families, and its celebratory spirit solidified the gratitude everyone felt for their PTA's generosity.

In addition to an increase in student engagement, Dr. Wehrmann's school also saw standardized test scores in reading improve. These achievement gains occurred while Minnesota's overall reading proficiency scores were decreasing.

Readers shouldn't have to rely on their teachers' garage sale skills or thrift store finds to reap the rewards of a high-quality, high-interest, and highly representative classroom library. They should rely on literacy leaders who prioritize these things in the budget.

Even if you don't oversee your school's budget, you can help others amplify student voice and use data to inform other aspects of the educational program. A culture of reading is one that transcends all subjects, departments, and instructional contexts (Jacobson, 2017). School assemblies are another opportunity to show readers our priorities.

Students in our school look forward to our annual Staff vs. Students Basketball game all year long. The game features 5th graders who take on teachers from around the school. To offset the height advantage teachers have, we assign zany challenges to the teachers' team. Things like carrying a heavy stack of homework for part of the game or wearing mittens always adds to the excitement. The tradition also includes a student who sings the National Anthem, a halftime show, and multiple camera crews, just like many professional sports experiences (see figure 2.8).

Figure 2.8: **Staff vs. Students Basketball Tradition**

To make literacy more of a priority during the event, we added a pop-up book fair outside and invited students to share booktalks at halftime. We also shared reading resources prepared for families in attendance. Students had a blast, and everyone walked away having heard a few book recommendations, too.

Chances are good that the traditions your school has scheduled happen because people throughout your organization already value them. From a strategic standpoint, finding ways to prioritize literacy within existing events is an efficient use of time and resources. Making meaningful changes to your budget and schedule can help jump-start your reading flow, but it also invites others in.

Connect reading to other high-interest activities: You need not invent additional work to jump-start your reading flow. In fact, sometimes the best way to create a culture of reading is to pay attention to the activities students are interested in outside of school. Unfortunately, this is not something school leaders have mastered yet.

Too often, we unroll new initiatives as separate silos. This can have the unintended effect of creating false dichotomies that push people to choose between a new thing and something they already value. Perhaps this is why only one in four change initiatives is successful (Anderson & James, 2020). Inviting people to choose between two things that are both important isn't really a choice.

I'll never forget the time one literacy leader told me they were working in a district that removed their library to create room for a Maker-Space. Honestly, I didn't believe it at first. It took a 20-30 minute conversation with the person to even begin to fathom how something like this could happen. As far as I could understand, the rationale behind the decision was that students and staff in the school would be able to walk to a nearby public library when they needed books. I'm sure there's more to the story, but the impact was that reading was pitted against innovation. I'll be the first person to advocate for tools and pedagogy that support opportunities for all students to collaborate, create, and invent their future. But *not* at the expense of growing readers.

> Inviting people to choose between two things that are both important isn't really a choice.

Schools should be looking for ways to connect reading to other high-interest activities, not replace it. I understand leaders need to make tough choices, but none of those choices should involve gutting a school's capacity to grow readers. I've said this before, but it's worth repeating. If anyone tries to tell you that you need to choose between books and a MakerSpace, do not believe them. Reading breathes new life into innovation, just as science, technology, and engineering enrich reading experiences. Literacy leaders create spaces for both.

We ordered books from several different genres to place on each of our school's Mobile MakerSpace carts (see figure 2.9). We have 18-20 of these carts containing everything from 3D printers and robotics to knitting looms and cardboard construction tools. Adding books to the carts has made it easier for students to take their passions and research deeper.

Another way we've connected reading to students' interests outside of school is by adding a dozen or so Build-A-Book stations to our media center (see figure 2.10). Anyone can check out the stations

Figure 2.9: **Strategically Placed Books on a MakerSpace Cart**

Figure 2.10: **Build-A-Book Stations**

and recreate themes and characters from their favorite books using LEGO bricks. Seeing students crowd around their LEGO board and talk about books while building with classmates always puts me in the reading flow zone. The Build-A-Book stations also demonstrate the connection between making and reading.

One of my favorite stories involving the Build-a-Book stations came when I overheard the conversation several 5th-grade boys were having. They were working together to recreate the cover for *Scar Island* by Dan Gemeinhart when an argument ensued. The debate was about what shade of LEGO bricks most aligned with some of the darker elements of the book's plot. It was one of the greatest conversations I've ever stumbled upon.

The result of our school creating this connection between books and making has been subtle, yet profound. Students who might otherwise be reluctant to read, speak, or engage in class are invited into experiences where they're more comfortable communicating. Nobody wants to be embarrassed in front of their peers; providing students alternatives to traditional reading activities can feel safer and more inclusive (Flachbart, 2019).

Another way I've seen reading connected to the activities and topics students enjoy is through Literacy-O-Lanterns. Each fall, our media center fills with 100+ painted pumpkins representing some of our students' favorite books. I always try to paint a half dozen or so pumpkins myself to jump-start the fun (see figure 2.11). The tradition helps me share my reading life with others, but if you go to #LiteracyOLanterns you can see what readers are painting in classrooms everywhere.

Reach out to an author or literacy mentor: Jump-starting your reading flow doesn't have to be a solo sport. Working with others to move forward

Figure 2.11: **#LiteracyOLanterns**

on a shared vision is an important aspect of strong leadership (Wallace Foundation, 2013). Not only that, connecting with authors and literacy leaders can enhance your own growth and create excitement schoolwide.

I'll never forget the year we invited several authors to help us kick-off a family booktalk project. Several authors sent us videos of themselves doing booktalks with their families. It was one of the coolest, most authentic things I've seen. One of my favorite video submissions came from Minh Lê. During his booktalk video, Minh's children interrupted him several times, mainly through laughter. It was impossible not to smile as I watched. And it was also the perfect booktalk for his book, *Let Me Finish!* (see figure 2.12).

We've also reached out to authors and other literacy leaders to help with a design-thinking experience we called "Lit Tank." We based the project on the hit-television show, *Shark Tank.* Instead of having sharks choose which student's reading invention they liked best, we empowered students to choose a literacy shark.

Figure 2.12: **Family BookTalk with Minh Lê**

Basically, we invited authors, librarians, publishers, and other literacy leaders to record short videos explaining a reading-related problem our students might be able to help solve. Then, students selected the video/problem they wanted to tackle (or identified their own problem to solve).

Seeing the authentic engagement of students as they responded to challenges presented by a global cadre of authors, librarians, and other literacy leaders was unlike anything I've experienced before. I don't think I left the reading flow zone for weeks after the experience. When an author or reading-role model can help, the experience can initiate so many things. But you must extend the invitation.

An Invitation to Jump-Start Your Reading Flow

Implementing some of the ideas in this chapter have helped me jump-start and sustain my motivation to read. And I think they could do the same for you. This activity (see figure 2.13) is an invitation to respond to what you've read in a manner that's meaningful to you and the readers you serve.

1. Review the four ways to jump-start your reading flow above. Then, choose one of the ways (A, B, C, or D) that you'd like to try to make a difference. Of course, you can always modify an idea or try something that makes more sense in your school.

2. Plan your approach. Focus on authentic invitations instead of big or flashy changes.

3. Commit to implementing your idea. Share your plans with other literacy leaders in our community of leaders at #LiteracyLever. You can seek advice, support others, and celebrate progress with us!

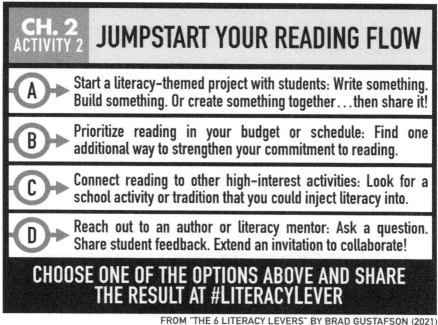

CH. 2 ACTIVITY 2 JUMPSTART YOUR READING FLOW

A ➤ Start a literacy-themed project with students: Write something. Build something. Or create something together...then share it!

B ➤ Prioritize reading in your budget or schedule: Find one additional way to strengthen your commitment to reading.

C ➤ Connect reading to other high-interest activities: Look for a school activity or tradition that you could inject literacy into.

D ➤ Reach out to an author or literacy mentor: Ask a question. Share student feedback. Extend an invitation to collaborate!

CHOOSE ONE OF THE OPTIONS ABOVE AND SHARE THE RESULT AT #LITERACYLEVER

FROM "THE 6 LITERACY LEVERS" BY BRAD GUSTAFSON (2021)

Figure 2.13: **Jumpstart Your Reading Flow (Activity)**

Questions to Push the Field Forward

+ Are there people in your sphere of influence who may not see themselves in the invitation(s) and work you're doing? How do you know? What steps will you take to lead a more inclusive reading community?
+ What are some things you can do right now to help students and colleagues find their reading flow?

Leverage Your Literacy Leadership Schoolwide

Sharing an authentic invitation with others requires you to have a *current and consistent* relationship with reading. I'm not just talking about reading professional literature or articles on leadership. Before you even attempt the schoolwide challenge below, be sure to commit to working on your reading flow.

The challenge is to share an authentic invitation while being on the lookout for invitations other literacy leaders might be sharing (see figure 2.14). As you're connecting with colleagues, ask for ideas about creating some type of shared reading experience in your school.

After that, commit to implementing the shared vision. Then, reflect on the experience and process. Seek input on how others felt included and use what you learn to inform future invitations you share.

CH. 2 ACTIVITY 3 SHARE AN INVITATION

SCHOOLWIDE IMPLEMENTATION CHALLENGE

1. **Start small – connect with colleagues organically**
2. **Ask for ideas about creating some type of shared reading experience in your school**
3. **Look for ways to authentically invite others into the conversation and work – be inclusive**
4. **Commit to implementing the shared vision**

"SURPRISE! IT'S A BOOK PARTY STACKED WITH ALL YOUR FAVORITE FRIENDS: A PICNIC OF WORDS + SOUNDS IN LEAPS + BOUNDS"
HOW TO READ A BOOK BY KWAME ALEXANDER

FROM "THE 6 LITERACY LEVERS" BY BRAD GUSTAFSON (2021)

Figure 2.14: **Schoolwide Implementation Challenge**

CHAPTER 3

The Walking Stick

I magine this: A few hours later, you're walking through the front doors of your favorite restaurant. You can't believe this is happening, but it was an invitation you couldn't pass up.

You're a little early, so you slide into a comfy chair in the lobby and wait. You glance out the windows half expecting to see Dayo holding a "Got you!" sign. A bigger part of you is wondering whether you should just leave.

The smell of spices and fresh citrus emanating from the kitchen convinces you to stay. In between expectant glances outside, you fumble through a mental list of questions you'd like to ask your mystery-reading-friend—or whatever the invitation said.

Your eyes widen when you notice your reading mentor approaching from a nearby booth. Before you have the chance to force out an awkward greeting, she smiles and shakes your hand. As you sit down, you notice there's a half-read book on the table. You imagine your friend stealing a few moments to read as she was waiting.

At first, you're surprised at how natural the conversation feels. Your friend is genuinely curious about your work and leadership. You find yourself wishing you could ask questions as engaging as the ones she's sharing. This doesn't stop you from finishing the story you started about the first chapter book you ever read. You're so immersed in the memory that your hand knocks over a walking stick somebody must've leaned against the edge of your table. Your eyebrows shoot up in surprise when your friend apologizes for placing it there. Without missing a beat, you reach down to retrieve the stick. As you turn it over in your hands you notice some carvings etched deep into the wood.

Your friend nods knowingly and says, "These are some of the questions I carry with me. They've evolved over time, but their essence remains the same."

With your mouth partly agape, you realize the questions that invigorated your conversation came from the walking stick. Just to be sure you ask, "So are these the same questions you ask everyone?"

Your friend takes a deep and thoughtful breath before responding. "Everyone has different needs. The questions I'm sharing with you help me to understand your story. Your beliefs about reading. And some of the things the readers you serve might need."

Without any further explanation, she takes a sip of water and invites you to finish the story you had started.

- What is the first chapter book or series you remember reading?
- Why is asking questions so important?
- What happens when the right questions are not being asked?
- When you think about the readers in your school, what questions might they be counting on you to ask?

WALKING STICK

LEVER #3

noun /waw-king stik/

1. A metaphor for the questions literacy leaders carry to initiate deeper conversations.

2. A tool to help you initiate conversation, lean into problematic practices, and push the field.

"The librarian leveraged the walking stick during an important conversation about books being challenged."

FROM "THE 6 LITERACY LEVERS" BY BRAD GUSTAFSON (2021)

Figure 3.1: **Walking Stick Defined**

"You can't teach what you don't know.
You can't lead where you won't go."

~Gary Howard

From Story to Practice

If you struggle to initiate meaningful conversation, how will you ever help move literacy practices forward? Questions are a reliable tool to initiate dialogue and enhance understanding. They're also a guiding force for change. Much like the walking stick your friend carried, leaning on the right questions can open up important dialogue.

You might be wondering what questions are the best. Honestly, it depends. It depends on the needs of your team. It also depends on the needs of the readers you serve. The limited vantage point I have does not equip me to know what questions your readers need you to be asking. This chapter will provide you some food for thought as you formulate the right questions, but ultimately, you and your team are the most qualified to make this decision. Just trust yourself as you're figuring it out.

Trusting yourself to figure it out while you're also trying to determine what literacy leadership looks like can be tough. Trust me when I tell you that showing up genuinely curious is half the battle. And doing this consistently makes all the difference in the world.

Curiosity and Consistency

A district administrator I used to work with would always wait for just the right moment to ask one very specific question. And she really pushed practice forward in the process. It didn't matter what we were discussing because her guiding question always seemed to apply to the work in which we were engaged. It never felt forced. It didn't matter if we were talking about policy, transportation, or summer school. She always found a way to genuinely ask one faithful question (or some variation of it):

> "How will our students with special needs be impacted?"
> "How does this decision affect students with special needs?"
> "How might we ensure students with special needs are included?"

After posing the question, she would listen with humility, observe, and support, as appropriate. Her steady leadership and thoughtful approach increased our capacity to lead in her absence. So much so that I still find myself trying to ask the right questions—including some of the same questions she asked—and it's been years since she retired. Talk about a legacy!

The Questions We Carry

The *right* questions are the ones that invite conversation, spur reflection, and challenge assumptions. The right questions for you and your team will reveal themselves with time. And with practice. To help you hone in on these, I'll share some of the questions other literacy leaders are asking (see figure 3.1). The questions were compiled through a combination of research and conversation with literacy leaders I respect.

Julie Kirchner is an inspiring library media specialist in Minnesota where I work. The questions Julie often asks are not only intentional,

5 QUESTIONS TO HELP INFORM YOUR LITERACY LEADERSHIP

1. **WILL THIS HELP OTHERS LEAN FURTHER INTO THEIR IDENTITY AS READERS?**

2. **HOW MIGHT WE MAKE THIS MORE AUTHENTIC AND INTRINSICALLY MOTIVATING?**

3. **IS THIS PRODUCING POSITIVE RESULTS AND TEACHING STUDENTS TO READ?**

4. **WOULD I CHOOSE THIS FOR MYSELF AS A READER?**

5. **WHO MIGHT NOT BE REPRESENTED IN THIS, AND IS ANYONE BEING MISREPRESENTED?**

FROM "THE 6 LITERACY LEVERS" BY BRAD GUSTAFSON (2021)
BISHOP, R. (1990), GABRIEL R. (2021), MELTZER, E. (2020), PAUL, A. (2021)
(J. KIRCHNER, PERSONAL COMMUNICATION, AUGUST 20, 2017)
(A. PAUL, PERSONAL COMMUNICATION, SEPTEMBER 28, 2021)

Figure 3.1: **Five Questions to Help Inform Your Literacy Leadership**

but they're enhanced by the thinking of countless other educators, authors, and experts from the field with whom she's connected.

Ashley Paul is another incredible leader and colleague. She's serving as a principal and her passion and commitment to helping each and every student succeed is unsurpassed. I asked her about some of the questions guiding her work and she was happy to share as well.

The result of the research and my conversations with both Ashley and Julie are a list of five questions to help inform your literacy leadership. If the list appears unclear or incomplete, that's probably because it is. These questions are conversation starters, and they shouldn't be the only questions you ask. But they can help you start to think about the walking stick you'd like to carry. These questions can be applied to a variety of situations a literacy leader might encounter. To make the questions fit your leadership context, simply replace the word "this" with a specific practice or decision. I share some examples of how each of the questions could be applied to different practices or decisions throughout this chapter.

Don't worry if my examples aren't perfectly aligned to the work you're leading. The goal is to help you see how questions can be leveraged to create conversation in *any* setting. The opportunities you find to ask questions are much more important than any example I could share. I do, however, need to point out the importance of *how* you ask questions.

Nothing shuts down a conversation like asking a colleague a loaded question. Or one you think you already know the answer to. Wielding questions as a weapon or as an explanation point does not build culture. It's just the opposite. The questions you carry as a literacy leader should be carried with curiosity.

There is a strong connection between curiosity and culture. Curiosity is the catalyst to conversation. Conversation inspires change. And even the smallest change can create culture. With this in mind, let's take a closer look at each of the five questions that can help you create culture.

Question #1: Will [this] help others lean further into their identity as readers?

When you ask, "Will this help others lean further into their identity as readers?" you create a space for the many aspects that go into a person's reading identity to be considered, from environmental factors supporting reading flow to a reader's interests, strengths, and skills they have yet to develop.

> There is a strong connection between curiosity and culture. Curiosity is the catalyst to conversation. Conversation inspires change.

Asking this question reduces the likelihood you and your team will unknowingly perpetuate practices that damage readers. It would be difficult to fathom any educator intentionally harming a reader. However, this is exactly what can happen when we focus on a single aspect of a reader's identity without being intentional in understanding more about the reader as a whole person.

Schools can overemphasize a student's reading skills at the expense of the other aspects of reading identity; attitude, self-efficacy, habits, book choice, and process (Scoggin & Schneewind; 2021). We do this when we refer to a reader as a "high flyer" or "low reader," but we also do it when we restrict their reading choices based on our own beliefs about reading.

A person's reading identity is typically formed at an early age, but reading identities are complex and formative (see figure 3.2). They are reinforced and disrupted by the practices and culture we create (Hall, 2014). By being more intentional at every level of leadership, we can nurture students' reading identities and confront practices doing damage to readers.

READING IDENTITY

noun /ree-ding ahy-den-ti-tee/

1. The skills, experiences, and stories a reader carries with them.
2. The complex and evolving behaviors, attitudes, and beliefs a reader brings to every experience.

"The teacher helped students lean into their reading identities by connecting them to book choices that included strong and powerful representation."

FROM "THE 6 LITERACY LEVERS" BY BRAD GUSTAFSON (2021)

Figure 3.2: **Reading Identity Defined**

When you fail to ask questions that center the reading identity of all students, you inevitably damage the identities of some. Damage that could take years to repair and restore.

When I was hired as a second-grade teacher, I joined a school with a robust online reading program already in place. The program attached short comprehension quizzes to books and assigned students points based on how well students scored after reading a book and testing. Let me tell you, I invested all my new-teacher heart and soul into that reading program. I created an enormous racetrack that spanned an entire wall in our school commons. I cut out paper race cars that had each student's "magic number" on the side of the car. With each comprehension quiz passed, their cars would progress along the wall. I even added prizes as incremental pit stops along the track.

Racing across the wall in our school commons, veering over light switches, under SmartBoards, and around door frames—those cars represented excellence in reading instruction. To me. But here's the thing that gets me—and I've got a lump in my throat just typing this—there were always a few students who struggled to get past the first power outlet on the wall. That outlet was right next to the starting line. And what I realize now, is that it served as an inhumane monument to all the readers who couldn't even read and test enough to earn five points.

Oh, how I talked myself into thinking I treated these readers with the same love, excitement, and encouragement that I approached my 100-point club with. I would read with the 5-point kids. Give them extra class time to take quizzes. And hold recess over their heads to "help" and motivate them, of course. Deep down, I always wondered why they wouldn't just read and take those tests. Because surely the thing that was wrong in this situation was them and not how I showed up as a teacher.

How wrong I was. If I could go back in time and ask myself one simple question, I would. In a heartbeat. And that question would NOT be whether I would want a reading-race track or computer points for myself. When the reading lives of students are involved, what I would choose for myself should not be the sole determining question that drives practice. I wish I had asked, *Will this help my students lean further into their identity as readers?* Because the answer for many of those precious babies was, "No!"

What I was doing was effectively reducing their reading identities to winners and losers represented by paper cars on a wall. I'm not sharing this story to try and right my conscience or convince you that certain reading programs are inherently good or bad. Any decision that is universally applied to *all* readers without being interrogated through the lens of *each and every* reader runs the risk of doing damage to *some* readers. This applies to curriculum, programs, and even how we recognize the accomplishments of readers.

I recently saw middle-school teacher and literacy expert Pernille Ripp share an idea she uses to build and celebrate readers at the end of the year. Her idea to provide readers the opportunity to reflect on individual growth and then celebrate that growth is a shining example of leading on behalf of every reader (see figure 3.3) in a manner that protects and affirms their reading identity. In the same social media post Pernille wrote, "So much of what we do comes down to kids feeling good on their reading journey, no matter where they are on it." (Ripp, 2021)

The more I think about Pernille's tweet, the more purposeful I want to be in planning awards ceremonies and announcements in the future. I imagine I've missed countless opportunities to support and

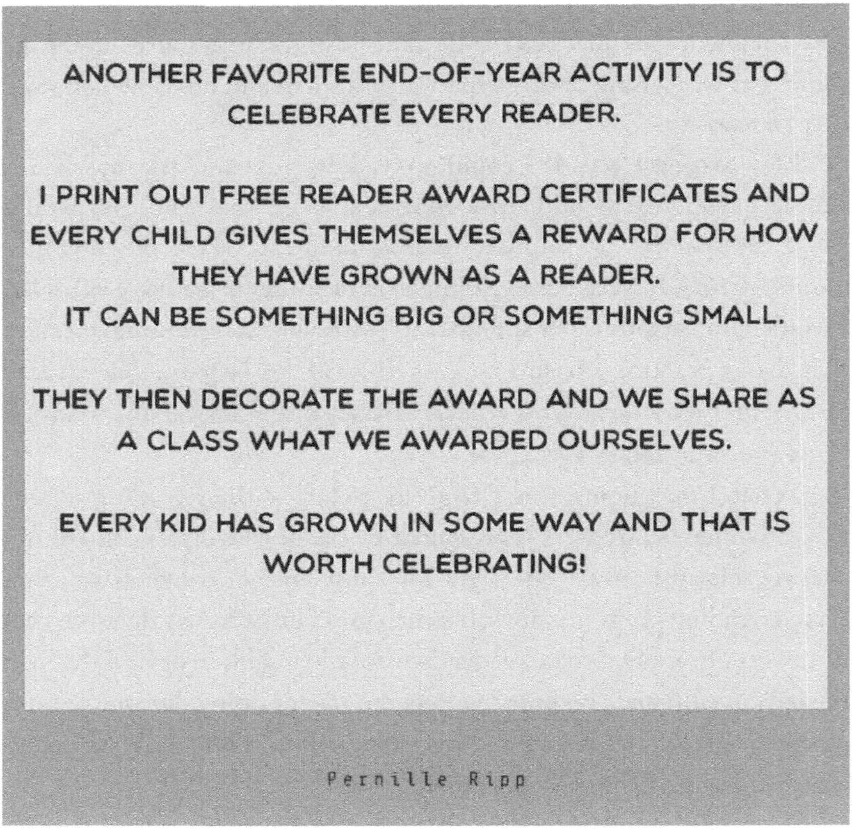

ANOTHER FAVORITE END-OF-YEAR ACTIVITY IS TO CELEBRATE EVERY READER.

I PRINT OUT FREE READER AWARD CERTIFICATES AND EVERY CHILD GIVES THEMSELVES A REWARD FOR HOW THEY HAVE GROWN AS A READER.
IT CAN BE SOMETHING BIG OR SOMETHING SMALL.

THEY THEN DECORATE THE AWARD AND WE SHARE AS A CLASS WHAT WE AWARDED OURSELVES.

EVERY KID HAS GROWN IN SOME WAY AND THAT IS WORTH CELEBRATING!

Pernille Ripp

Figure 3.3: **Celebrating Each and Every Reader**

protect students' reading identities over the years. No matter what questions you've failed to ask in the past, the future is full of countless decision-making moments when you can ask, "Will this help others lean further into their identity as readers?"

Question #2: *How might we make [this] more authentic and intrinsically motivating?*

When you ask, "How might we make this more authentic and intrinsically motivating?" you're inviting dialogue. Dialogue that could make reading, and the tasks you tie to it, more authentic and relevant to readers.

As a system, the decisions we've made about reading are not having the impact any of us would want. Students' attitudes towards academic reading become more negative over the course of a school year (Pak & Weseley, 2012). Perhaps more alarming is how students' motivation to read decreases the more they read classical literature (Locher et al., 2019). Many readers don't appreciate the artificial practices schools tie to their reading lives (Locher et al., 2019).

Travis Crowder is a high school English teacher and author who is trying to work toward more authentic versions of literary conversations. Several years ago, he started telling students they were not allowed to raise their hands while they discussed a text. If they wanted to say something, they needed to formulate their ideas, wait for someone to finish speaking, and then share their thoughts. To scaffold these authentic conversations, Travis and his classes talk about the difference between "right there" questions and the value of open-ended and analytical questions.

Travis also provides students time to generate questions prior to discussing a text. The first few times are wobbly because students are not accustomed to authentic conversations about texts, so Travis is intentional in coming back to the practice with additional texts. The result of this work has been deeper conversations about text which are essentially deeper and more authentic conversations about life.

Conversations are not the only thing literacy leaders design to be authentic and intrinsically motivating. Jennifer Cherry is an English language arts teacher in Virginia who wants students to be able to respond to their reading in authentic and motivating ways. She invited them to create Netflix-inspired screen designs based on their favorite books and authors. When I first saw her students' Bookflix reading graphics, I knew I needed to create my own—which speaks to the power of intrinsic motivation (see figure 3.4). As I was drafting the short synopsis for my Bookflix image, I thought about how different the process felt compared to some of the traditional summaries and reports I was required to do throughout my formal education. The activity even motivated me to research more books by Alan Gratz. And maybe that's the point. School should make students want to binge read.

Figure 3.4: **Bookflix Graphic**

Figure 3.5: **Book-Bento Boxes**

My good friend, Jenn LaGarde, teaches university classes for educators aspiring to be teacher-librarians. She shared a Book-Bento Box project she's used in her Young-Adult Literature course (see figure 3.5). Bento Boxes are traditional Japanese boxed meals that usually contain a single portion of food that's beautifully arranged in a compact box.

Jenn needed her students to complete a summative assessment involving a book they'd read but wanted it to be in a format that they could replicate in their classrooms. She also wanted it to be intrinsically motivating for university students to complete. She started by providing some background on Bento Boxes so her class could appreciate the context and beauty of them. After that, she invited everyone to reflect on items they might include in their Book-Bento Boxes as they were reading. Some students kept a journal to assist with this. Then, students conversed with a classmate or teacher to try and narrow down their ideas to only those they would include in the box. Last, students were invited to photograph and/or share their boxes with others.

I fell in love with the idea because it felt more authentic than some of the other assessments I've seen. I also thought about how Book-Bento Boxes could be used as a background building experience *before* reading a book. As I was chatting with Jenn about how we might make the assignments we attach to reading more authentic and motivating to students, she shared a powerful perspective that I've paraphrased below:

> *Moving beyond book reports and reading logs involves more than finding new replacements. It's about asking the questions that draw us closer to what robust readers actually do. I created a personal Padlet that documents my personal reading life. Many other readers use GoodReads to connect to a community of readers while responding to a text they've just read. So, my question is, "Are we willing to provide students opportunities to engage in similar activities?" These are some of the things we should be thinking about, even if it means co-creating new spaces or inventing new approaches that they're intrinsically motivated to engage with (J. LaGarde, Personal Communication, June 23, 2020).*

A Word of Caution

It's important to keep in mind that just because a reader wouldn't choose something doesn't mean it's unimportant. Children tend to choose tasks they can do. They are less likely to appreciate the practice and repetition required of learning challenging tasks like learning to read (Meltzer, 2020). Do not make your sole litmus test for literacy leadership decisions dependent on whether something is intrinsically motivating to everyone.

The other thing to keep in mind is that trying to make a practice more motivating doesn't mean the practice was beneficial to begin with. This is where something I refer to as Shiny Book Report Syndrome (S.B.R.S.) comes into play (see figure 3.6). S.B.R.S. refers to polishing up the traditional book report to the point it appears shiny, new, or motivating. However, just because something is shiny, new, or has been injected with additional relevance doesn't guarantee it's good for readers.

S.B.R.S. could apply to virtually any literacy leadership decision you make. It is not limited to classroom practices. Updating a less-effective approach by applying a pop-culture theme doesn't make it more authentic or worthwhile. You need to pursue what is purposeful, meaningful, and important to the readers you serve.

Making Things More Authentic and Motivating

Sometimes the little things turn out to be the big things. Little to us, but big to them. I remember when a student in our elementary school

FROM "THE 6 LITERACY LEVERS" BY BRAD GUSTAFSON (2021)

Figure 3.6: **Shiny Book Report Syndrome Defined**

wrote a book and shared it with our media specialist. The book was fantastic, and somebody had the idea to add it to our media collection. We worked with a company to have the book printed and bound which also allowed us to order an extra copy to share with our local public library.

Once the hardcover version of the book arrived, we couldn't keep it on our shelves! In fact, the waiting list for the book dwarfed the waiting lists for some of the year's hot-new releases from children's and Y.A. authors around the world. This was a very big deal to our student-author. The entire experience had a level of authenticity that the traditional publishing process and curriculum doesn't always provide. And it started with teacher-leaders noticing a student's passion for writing and asking, *How might we make this more authentic and intrinsically motivating?*

This same question can also be applied to the professional learning we plan for adults. I was at a literacy event in Florida where participants were invited to share book recommendations. The event organizers created a game to remove some of the pressure people can feel when sharing book recommendations in front of others. They injected an element of game play into the book recommendations people were sharing. The game involved trying to add random words into book recommendations without others knowing which unrelated word(s) you added. I immediately noticed how the activity reduced the self-induced pressure I was feeling to give the perfect booktalk. As the room erupted with laughter, conversation, and engagement, I sensed the game was having a similar effect on others. Talk about purposeful!

Game play can be an authentic and motivating way to practice a skill while also building culture, whether you're planning a family literacy night, reading workshop, or your next staff meeting. The conversation and laughter that often accompanies games can be authentic and motivating. But more than that, it demonstrates how applying a guiding question to a practice can improve the experience for some readers.

In case you're interested in bringing the game itself to your classroom or school, I've included directions and a template (see figure 3.7).

1. Find a partner or small group to share a book recommendation with.
2. Start by selecting one or two random words from a basket. You could use the random words provided or create your own.
3. Do not tell anyone else your random words. Half the fun is trying to guess your partner's random words after they're done sharing their book recommendation.
4. Next, share your book recommendation with your partner or small group. The goal is to sneak your random words into your book recommendation in a way that makes sense, no matter how out-of-context the word you drew might seem.
5. After you share your book recommendation, provide your partner the opportunity to guess what your random words were.

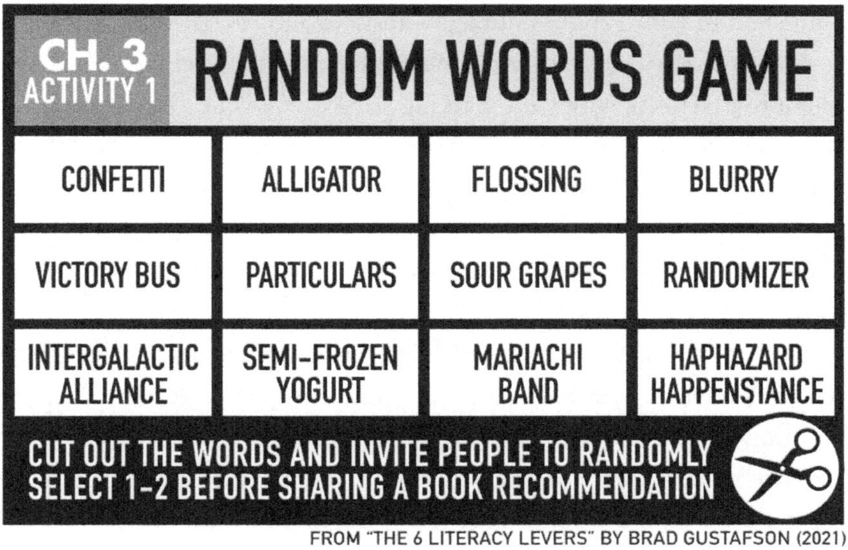

CH. 3 ACTIVITY 1 — RANDOM WORDS GAME

CONFETTI	ALLIGATOR	FLOSSING	BLURRY
VICTORY BUS	PARTICULARS	SOUR GRAPES	RANDOMIZER
INTERGALACTIC ALLIANCE	SEMI-FROZEN YOGURT	MARIACHI BAND	HAPHAZARD HAPPENSTANCE

CUT OUT THE WORDS AND INVITE PEOPLE TO RANDOMLY SELECT 1-2 BEFORE SHARING A BOOK RECOMMENDATION

FROM "THE 6 LITERACY LEVERS" BY BRAD GUSTAFSON (2021)

Figure 3.7: **Random Words Game (Activity)**

81

I suggest modeling how the game works after reading the rules. Here is an example using *Granted* by John David Anderson. The random words I drew were *alligator* and *confetti* but don't tell anyone my words if you're using this to model how to play. Here's my book recommendation containing the random words I drew:

> *"Have you ever thought about what happens when you throw a penny in a wishing well or make a wish on a shooting star? Imagine how you would feel if you discovered the magic involved in making dreams come true. I cried **alligator** tears when I read, Granted, by John David Anderson because it revealed how a hidden world of fairies responds to each and every wish we make. I promise you'll want to throw **confetti** after discovering the secret world of wishes and reading this magical book about the fairies who make them come true."*

Some readers enjoy games. Others may aspire to have their writing published in your school's library—and beyond. What feels authentic and intrinsically motivating to one reader may not feel the same way to another. This is why your walking stick carries questions instead of activities and assignments. Try to remember that reading for the sake of reading is one of the most authentic things we can promote in schools.

Question #3: *Is [this] producing positive results and teaching students to read?*

When you ask, "Is this producing positive results and teaching students to read?" you're leading for relationships and results. Because building relationships is only part of the work.

The results you're looking for could also include increasing reading motivation and book access. They might be reflected in increased attendance at family literacy nights or updating your school's media collection to ensure its books are more representative of all students.

These things are important and represent very real results. However, I'm going to make an intentional pivot away from culture-building practices and focus on something slightly different: The skill of reading.

The overarching purpose of reading instruction is to teach students to read (Meltzer, 2020). Therefore, the mission of literacy leaders is to create the conditions that ensure a literacy-rich environment in which every student learns to read. If students are not learning to read, it is your responsibility to ask questions that determine why (Gabriel, 2021). And to respond accordingly.

Here's a scenario to consider. Imagine a child who is struggling to read and has been for years. You probably don't need to see her latest standardized test scores to know she's struggling. You've heard her try to read. In class and in the hallway. It's laborious. The perplexing thing is you know she's been surrounded by a print-rich environment at home and at school. She's in 4th grade now, but the discrepancy between her reading skills and those of her classmates is significant. The reading intervention support you felt so sure would be her saving grace hasn't helped her crack the reading code yet. The same services that once sounded like just the right thing to help get her *on* track now seem like they have become *a* track.

Despite this struggle, her positive attitude and motivation to learn seem undaunted. Sure, there have been a couple of times where she appeared to be a little more self-conscious being pulled from her classroom to receive the additional support. But for the most part, she's as dialed in today as she was the first day she qualified for reading intervention several years ago.

I share this stripped-down scenario because it points to the urgency of the question, *Is this producing positive results and teaching students to read?* It's a question that needs to be asked frequently, at every level of leadership. We cannot be satisfied with simply creating a motivation to read while leaving some readers without the requisite skills required to do so.

Creating a culture of reading requires you to ensure students learn how to read. I've been on a journey to learn more about this aspect of literacy leadership the past several years. I'll summarize a few of the key research findings, but you will want to do a deeper dive. Struggling through some of the more nuanced and polarizing aspects of reading instruction has been a growth-inducing process for me. The goal of this chapter is to help you leverage questions to increase your effectiveness and not purport to have all the answers.

Reading requires a person to connect symbols to sounds and written words to meanings. These skills are not intuitive and do not naturally occur as a child grows older (Goodwin, 2020; Moats, 1999). This is drastically different from how children learn to talk. Students need to be taught how to decode the printed word and translate it into meaning (Allington, 2013; Goodwin, 2020). A print-rich environment alone doesn't ensure students will learn to read. It doesn't work to assume a student will just catch up—or that things will eventually start to click—as time passes. Students need explicit instruction. But they also need literacy leaders committed to making sure each student receives the instruction needed to crack the reading code.

This code-focused instruction that's based on letters and sounds is critical. But it doesn't exist apart from meaning-focused instruction that involves vocabulary, context, and communication patterns (Gabriel, 2021). Systematically and successfully ensuring the two are integrated might be where you and your team do their most important work. Asking questions about the impact and results of practice will help you get there.

Question #4: *Would I choose [this] for myself as a reader?*

When you ask, "Would I choose this for myself as a reader?" you're practicing The Golden Rule of Reading: *Assign unto others as you'd like assigned unto you.* You're also asking a question that is very accessible to teams. Because most people are comfortable telling you about the things they like and don't like.

This question also allows you to initiate conversations about reading preferences without anyone having to worry about wrong answers. It can also serve as a safe way to push practice by considering the preferences and perspective of readers through your eyes.

If you enjoy having choice and input with what you're reading... students might, too. If you wouldn't like being restricted by a label or number...students may not appreciate it, either. This question applies to literacy practices just as much as it applies to the professional learning experiences you might be planning for others.

Matthew Arend is a principal in Texas who understands how forcing faculty to read something they aren't invested in can leave a bad taste in anybody's mouth. His team invested a portion of their Title I budget to purchase books for use in a staff book-tasting experience. Matthew and his team set-up their library like a restaurant and invited teachers to sample books before they selected what they wanted to read (see figure 3.8).

The menu included several courses to whet everyone's appetite, and titles ranged from books with an instructional focus to books that challenged and inspired. One of the highlights from the experience came from a teacher who approached him afterwards and said she had already talked with a colleague about setting up a book tasting for students. And that's the *Golden Rule of Reading* in action during a professional learning experience.

You don't need a lot of fanfare to lead reading experiences that you would choose for yourself. I know another principal who started planning for her faculty book study by collecting feedback from teachers on the books they were interested in discussing together. Then, the principal asked the authors of the books to record short video greetings. The videos also included take-aways from the books that helped teachers decide what book was best for them.

Each of the principals above amplified the voices of readers in different ways. They were also intentional about planning professional

Figure 3.8: **Staff Book-Tasting Experience**

learning experiences that they would choose for themselves. Whether you're providing literacy leadership to a district-wide book study, within the walls of your classroom, or in a library, being mindful of the things that motivate *you* as a reader will help you be more effective as you strive to *do unto others*. Reading motivation matters.

Reading motivation is a strong predictor of reading behavior (Locher et al., 2019). Reading motivation is closely connected to reading for pleasure. The simple, yet profound, act of reading for pleasure creates caring and compassionate people, increases student achievement in multiple subjects, and correlates positively with overall success in adulthood (Allington, 2012; Hiebert & Reutzel, 2010; Djikic & Oatley, 2014; Simonton, 1988; Sullivan & Brown, 2013).

Asking what you would choose as a reader will help you be more cognizant of the role reading motivation plays in your decisions. It doesn't guarantee you'll make decisions that other readers would choose for themselves, but it should spur additional reflection and conversation.

Question #5: *Who might not be represented in [this] and is anyone being misrepresented?*

When you ask, "Who might not be represented and is anyone being misrepresented?" you're providing leadership that supports every reader you serve. And in many ways, you're asking one of the most important questions you can ask. If the work you're doing doesn't include everyone, it's not good enough for anyone. All students have a right to see themselves represented in the books they're reading in positive, inspiring, and authentic ways (Bishop, 1990). This isn't something that's only important to some readers; it matters to all readers. Without access to books that represent the true diversity in our world, readers from dominant social groups miss important opportunities to see the beauty and stories in others (Bishop, 1990).

As a teacher-leader, Ashley Paul spent hours working with her team to research books that represented all readers. Her school invested in books for every classroom and used a book-of-the-month format to introduce the texts. Over time, they developed lesson plans that incorporated the use of Thinking Maps and discussion questions to support deeper conversation. The lesson plans and accompanying questions were differentiated based on grade-level ranges.

As comprehensive as Ashley and her team's work with curating representative books was, they noticed another important question they needed to start asking. One of the books they chose to feature for the book-of-the-month seemed like an important fit. It was a heartwarming story about gratitude and the importance of family. The main character was a Black boy who lived with his grandmother and couldn't afford the popular shoes other kids were wearing at the time. In the end, he realized that he had much to be grateful for, despite the socio-economic situation he and his family were living with.

As Ashley read the book to her kindergarten students at the time, she realized the theme and characters in the book were reinforcing an age-old narrative that Black kids (and boys, in particular) are either poor or from broken homes. After reading the book with students, she struggled to undo the unintended damage it may have caused to all students. Truth be told, this was the narrative she lived growing up, and one that she was consistently embarrassed about when her classmates would comment on it.

Ashley's courageous leadership, learning, and vulnerability in sharing make it possible for you and me to ask additional questions. Because a focus on finding representative books, or books with characters students can identify with in terms of race and culture, isn't enough. We also need to examine whether anyone is being misrepresented and think about why this is problematic.

Your Literacy Legacy

As I already mentioned, I'm not here to tell you the specific questions you and your team need to ask. I do want to help by encouraging you to carry questions your readers and school need you to be asking. When you do this consistently, your legacy will be connected to the success of the readers you serve.

Legacy. The word itself sounds grandiose, but a *legacy* isn't about the person who creates it. It's about what we empower others to do. The same goes for a literacy legacy (see figure 3.9). A literacy legacy is about the capacity, culture, and hope we leave. It's also about the growth-inducing levers we share with others and the questions they will eventually carry.

> A literacy legacy is your gift to others. The gift you and your team co-create for kids.

LITERACY LEGACY

noun   /lit-er-uh-see leg-uh-see/

1. A gift given to readers through a series of small and intentional steps taken over a period of time.

2. The culture of reading you help create and leave for readers.

"The literacy legacy left by the librarian was forged from the example he set and the thoughtful questions, conversations, and decisions he made."

FROM "THE 6 LITERACY LEVERS" BY BRAD GUSTAFSON (2021)

Figure 3.9: **Literacy Legacy Defined**

A literacy legacy is your gift to others. The gift you and your team co-create for kids. Through consistent steps and culture-building conversations. To make this gift meaningful, readers need to be centered in the work. Your ability to articulate what this looks, sounds, and feels like is important. Taking time to think about the legacy you want to leave someday will help you determine the questions you should start asking today. For this activity (see figure 3.10), try to think about the things you hope readers see, hear, and feel when they are in your classroom and school.

1. With a reader-centric mindset, reflect on the things you hope all readers get to see.

2. Write down some of the things you expect to see in the row labeled, "Looks Like."

CH. 3 ACTIVITY 2	YOUR LITERACY LEGACY
LOOKS LIKE	▸ Books students can see themselves in. ▸ ▸
SOUNDS LIKE	▸ Students are centered in staff conversations. ▸ ▸
FEELS LIKE	▸ Comfortable...Authentic...Reading for Pleasure ▸ ▸

FROM "THE 6 LITERACY LEVERS" BY BRAD GUSTAFSON (2021)

Figure 3.10: **Your Literacy Legacy (Activity)**

3. Next, reflect on what you want reading to sound like. Challenge yourself to also think about what the professional conversations colleagues are having could sound like as well.

4. Write down some of the things you hope others might hear in the row labeled, "Sounds Like."

5. After that, reflect on how you hope all readers feel and write down some of these things in the row labeled, "Feels Like." This reflection could encompass feelings about the learning environment, books, conversations, policies, and reading.

6. Review your list with a colleague and ask them about the things they want all readers to see, hear, and feel. Then, decide what questions need to be asked to create these conditions. Start asking them.

I've shared how questions can be leveraged to help all readers succeed using a variety of examples. Big and small. From budgeting and professional development to intervention and classroom practice. The goal of sharing these examples was to highlight how carrying questions can help push practice forward. Just imagine what can happen if you become fluent in asking a variety of questions to initiate conversation and activate change! The final pages of this chapter provide you an opportunity to do just that. I will focus on a specific practice and peel back some of the problematic layers of that practice. I'll introduce some questions along the way, but the goal is for you to be able to read through my riff on reading logs and take time to wonder. Be curious. Maybe even jot down a few questions you could see yourself asking in the margin.

A Riff on Reading Logs

When was the last time you finished a book and desperately wanted to log about it? There are few things that suck the joy out of reading like mandatory reading logs.

At their best, reading logs can help readers track and reflect on what they're reading. Reading logs can also be a tool to support conversation with teachers about what students are reading (Ferlazzo, 2019). At their worst, reading logs are a forced and artificial accountability mechanism that restrict and control readers. Somewhere in the middle of the road, reading logs can be a tool to help encourage consistent reading, but the impact is seldom as positive as this might sound.

Our youngest child, Finn, was motivated by many things growing up. Books were *not* one of them. Despite the fact that the bookshelves in his bedroom had more books than a small indie bookstore, he just wanted to play. There was a time when my wife and I wondered whether Finn would *ever* take an interest in reading. It wasn't until he was introduced to the world of graphic novels that his appreciation for books began to grow. I recall him reading and re-reading the *Dog Man* series for hours on end. He eventually became so enamored with Dav Pilkey's style that he started dabbling with writing his own graphic novels.

When we sent our son to school the following year, we desperately hoped his teachers and new classmates would see his emerging passion for reading for the precious gift it was. And protect it. At the very least, we expected our son would return home each day in the same condition we sent him to school. He was sent home with a reading log instead.

At first, we dutifully signed these reading logs. However, it didn't take long for Finn's relationship with books to change. Watching him read and list the titles of books that "counted" on his log was painful. Instead of being intrinsically motivated to read, it was as though he was begrudgingly punching a timeclock. The scariest moment for me came when the reading embers that had started to glow just weeks before appeared to be dying.

I'm not proud of the series of questionable decisions our family made as this was playing out. Instead of asking how we might make the reading logs more authentic and motivating, we resorted to shortcuts and forgery. It started with auto-filling in the minutes on Finn's reading logs since we knew he was reading more than we reported—even if all the books didn't "count." Eventually, we trained Finn's older sister to initial his logs. When this didn't feel right, I placed an order for a customized rubber stamp (see figure 3.11).

After the custom stamp arrived in the mail, I realized I must've been having *a moment* the evening I ordered it. The text I chose was snarky and my son's teacher deserved much better. I retired the stamp before ever officially using it. But I knew something needed to change.

I racked my brain trying to find a way to approach our son's teacher without coming across as judgmental. It turns out, all I needed to do was initiate a conversation using one unassuming question: "How might we make this more authentic and intrinsically motivating for Finn?"

Our conversation only lasted 5-10 minutes, but during that time we were able to talk about a few of the concerning reading behaviors we had noticed since our son had been assigned reading logs. I listened with curiosity as his teacher shared her goals for Finn as a reader as

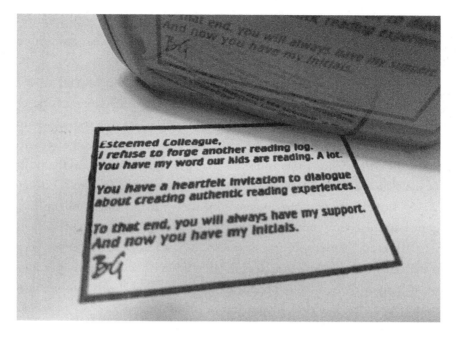

Figure 3.11: **Retired Reading Log Stamp**

well as some district expectations she was also trying to honor. Leading with purposeful questions and genuine curiosity helped us partner on a plan that felt more authentic to everyone involved. Finn's teacher made his reading logs optional, a choice that research supports.

Students who are issued voluntary logs do not experience the same level of decreasing motivation as those who are assigned mandatory logs (Pak & Weseley, 2012). In case you're interested, another strategy to make reading logs more meaningful is to embed engaging prompts, questions, and talking points for families to interact with in the logs. This can help mitigate *some* of the adverse effects of mandatory reading logs (Bailey et al., 2004). This wasn't the direction we decided to go, however.

Finn started submitting a weekly video talking about a few of the books he was reading. The one-minute videos helped his teacher get to

know him more as a reader while also satisfying a school-wide requirement pertaining to accountability and test scores. We also eradicated
the idea of books "not counting."

Finn's motivation to read gradually returned and he eventually delved
into several other series and genres. As an added bonus, the decision to
allow him to create short videos helped our son move one step closer to
his goal of becoming a *YouTuber*. He was empowered to interact with
books he chose, using tools and skills that were relevant beyond the walls
of his classroom, which was authentic and motivating to him (Brunow
2016). Looking back, I can only imagine how horrible things might have
gone had I used that snarky stamp or failed to show up with curiosity.

If literacy leaders don't ask questions and don't dive deeper into
potentially problematic practices, who will? Who will dive deeper into
what happens when we haphazardly distill reading down to one inau-
thentic practice, like documentation or proof of reading?

Reading logs (and other well-intentioned practices that are not
critically examined) can be problematic for a number of reasons. For
starters, they often give us false positives. You may see some readers
thrive while missing the damage the same practice is doing to others.
And just because some families appear to tolerate reading logs doesn't
mean they aren't creating unnecessary friction in others. Another problem is found in the invisible cost of reading logs. Missed opportunities.
Deeper discussion that never happens. And the conversations being
cut-off from kids.

I remember one summer, my wife and I had one of our kids create a
list of all the things she wanted to do over vacation. She had been pep-
pering us with questions and we were overwhelmed with everything
she was asking to do. We told her the list would be the best way to
communicate with us what her hopes and dreams were for the day,
week, and summer months. Whether she wrote down a bike ride or
nature walk, the list empowered her to organize her hopes and dreams
without forcing us to plan every second of our day. Or so we thought.

The list was actually a disaster. During an unfiltered conversation filled with plenty of tears, our daughter told us how she was feeling dismissed. She viewed the list as a tool that cut-off conversation. It made her feel less seen. Less heard. And it was the opposite of empowerment.

If we're not extremely careful, reading logs and other assignments can cut deeper conversations off. And not just between readers and their teachers. Conversations with classmates. And the empathy-building connections everyone can make in a classroom where books are being discussed. Forcing kids to list the books or minutes they're reading doesn't give these conversations a chance to happen. Conversation isn't the only compromise being made when we reduce reading to a log or other requirement.

Reading is a relationship. It doesn't start with an initiative, packet, or program. It starts with a consistent connection to books. Reading logs can damage this connection in several ways. The rules and feelings readers associate with reading logs can blur with how they view reading itself. The more they see reading as an accountability exercise, the more we risk damaging their long-term relationships with books. This leads to kids who know how to read but choose not to. As Kylene Beers would say, *"If we teach a child to read but fail to develop a desire to read, we will have created a skilled non-reader. A literate illiterate."*

> Reading is a relationship. It doesn't start with an initiative, packet, or program. It starts with a consistent connection to books.

Reading logs can be problematic from an equity standpoint as well. I don't think I need to explain how demanding the schedules of some families have become. Or how varied the support can look from one family to another. Some students are relied upon to care for siblings after school. Others are engaged with extra-curricular activities and volunteering commitments that make it difficult to start homework at a reasonable hour. Not to mention the homework they have in other classes.

When we overlook the uneven burden placed upon students and their families, it's easy to miss the damage reading logs might be doing to some students. Unknowingly forcing a student to choose between reading-related requirements, their family, team, sleep, or any number of other things will create winners and losers. Providing protected reading time during the day to all students would be one way to ensure every reader is supported.

Instead, inequitable practices that promote accountability and control are the norm. But it doesn't have to be this way. Asking questions about potentially harmful practices and identifying ideas to help readers interact in a more meaningful manner, is something you can start doing today (Locher, Becker & Pfost, 2019).

Ideas You Can Implement

I already mentioned how making reading logs optional would make a big difference. I want to share a few additional ideas from literacy leaders who are striving to make reading more authentic and meaningful. The ideas are not intended to take the place of important questions and conversations needing to be had. If anything, they should spur additional questions.

A team I work with has been engaged in deeper conversation about reading logs for years. Their conversations started with questions about what's authentic to readers but has grown into so much more. Instead of requiring students to record the number of books or minutes they've read in a log, the team uses different strategies throughout the year. One idea involves inviting students to contribute a paper-chain link to a class or grade-level chain each day they have a positive experience with a book (see figure 3.12).

Figure 3.12: **Reading Links**

The team also provides students protected reading time and is careful to use other onramps to conversation about students' books and lives. Hat tip to the incredible team of 3rd grade teachers who have led these conversations and work: Ashley Drill, Turi Hembre, Christina Skoglund, Jamie Tewksbury, and Genelle Weinbrenner.

Travis Crowder puts a unique spin on a practice inspired by Penny Kittle. He invites his high school students to create artistic notebook spreads to capture their thinking while reading. Sometimes they do this quickly and other times it's more deliberate. Unlike reading logs, notebook spreads shift the focus from *proof of* reading to *appreciation for* reading as students go back to a text multiple times in search of language that's beautiful, important, or necessary.

He occasionally invites students to re-read chapters in search of sentences that stand out to them. As they're doing this, they mark them lightly with a pencil or sticky note. Then, they take the language they're collecting and create highly visual spreads in their notebooks using magazines, pastels, and sketches to develop a deeper understanding (see figures 3.13 and 3.14).

No matter how students approach their notebook spreads (e.g., artistic spread, linguistic spread, multi-media spread), it's important to strike a balance between providing uninterrupted journaling time with some reflective turn & talks and class discussion to help students articulate why they selected certain language. This helps ensure notebook spreads aren't just another tool that eventually shuts down conversation. Travis is also careful not to overuse or over manage the notebook spreads. Doing so could cause them to become something students have little interest in owning.

Some 4th grade teachers I get to work with made reading logs more meaningful using reading legacy boards (see figure 3.15). The teachers invite students to save electronic images of books they enjoy in a document each reader prints near the end of the school year. Students use a clear acrylic paint to affix the book cover montage to pieces of scrap wood provided by their teachers. They also attach a photo of themselves reading to the opposite side of the board.

The legacy boards are a motivating time capsule that help students reflect on their interests and identity as readers. Best of all, they don't require forged signatures from families. Hat tip to Jon Zetah and Nate Nguyen for transforming traditional reading logs into an experience students and families value.

Questions to Push the Field Forward

- What would school look like if we carried a walking stick that helped us confront potentially damaging practices with curiosity and questions?
- It's difficult to push anything forward without trust. Are there impediments to honest dialogue and productive discourse you need to address?

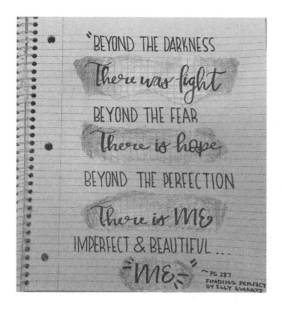

Figures 3.13 and 3.14: **Notebook Spread Examples**

Figure 3.15: **Reading Legacy Boards**

Leverage Your Literacy Leadership Schoolwide

Like a reliable walking stick, leaning on the questions your school needs you to ask will take your team further, deeper, and closer to the authentic reading experiences you want every reader to have. But questions need to include everyone.

Challenge yourself to connect with students to learn more about what matters to them (see figure 3.16). What are they hoping for from their reading experiences? What do they dream about, and to what degree do the books and other resources in your school reflect those dreams? Find out what's frustrating them or preventing them from wanting to read as well.

CH. 3
ACTIVITY 3 CARRY SCHOOLWIDE QUESTIONS

SCHOOLWIDE IMPLEMENTATION CHALLENGE

1. **Start small – ask readers what their literacy hopes, dreams, and frustrations are**

2. **Connect with colleagues to brainstorm several questions that center the voices of readers**

3. **Synthesize and refine 2–3 of the questions and practice carrying them collectively**

"SHE ASKS LOTS OF QUESTIONS. HOW COULD SHE RESIST? IT'S ALL IN THE HEART OF A YOUNG SCIENTIST."
ADA TWIST, SCIENTIST BY ANDREA BEATY

FROM "THE 6 LITERACY LEVERS" BY BRAD GUSTAFSON (2021)

Figure 3.16: **Schoolwide Implementation Challenge**

Then, work with your colleagues to brainstorm a list of questions that center the voices of readers. Don't make assumptions about what you think students mean or try to explain away what they shared. Use their input and stories to fuel your commitment.

Synthesize and refine the questions your colleagues brainstormed until you come up with 2-3 polished questions. The questions don't need to be perfect. And they certainly won't be the only ones you ask. They're just a starting point and stake in the ground for everyone in your school to leverage. At some point, we've got to look in the mirror and either *own* or *end* the practices preventing a culture of reading from taking root.

CHAPTER 4

The Utility Knife

Imagine this: You're still surprised you missed seeing the walking stick your friend had carried into the restaurant. However, there's no missing the small utility knife that's now sitting in the middle of the table. Mostly because your friend is gently tapping its iconic red handle.

Once. Twice. After three taps she removes her finger and produces a book. Then she starts to tell you why she thinks you'd enjoy it. It sounds captivating, really. You've had people recommend books before, but at this moment you've never felt so seen. Suddenly your friend smiles and places the red utility knife on top of the book. With a subtle flick of the finger, she slides them towards you and says, "Booktalks are the Swiss-Army knives of literacy leadership." You can't resist picking up the book and exploring its features.

You look back up after a few seconds—or at least what felt like a few seconds—only to realize your friend is gone. You crane your neck to scan the restaurant. Then, you do a double take because you'd recognize those purple highlights anywhere. It's the young woman from the café. And she's next to—*is that Dayo?!*

When they get to your table, Dayo introduces you to Lydia. She's wearing a screen-printed T-shirt that says, "I SLAY READING

103

LOGS." You aspire to be that cool someday. Although it can't be a coincidence they're both here at the same time you're meeting with your literacy mentor. You scan the restaurant again before inviting Dayo and Lydia to sit down.

Dayo doesn't waste any time. "Do tell...do tell!" he says.

"This meeting has been life-changing..." You gesture to the book and utility knife your friend gave you before disappearing.

Dayo instinctively asks, "What did she say about the book?" You tilt your head to the side and offer him an inquisitive look. Dayo adds, "Book lovers always share booktalks. It's a thing."

You smile as you recall the heartfelt words your friend had shared with you about the book. It was definitely a thing. Reliving the excitement of your friend's book recommendation reminds you of a question. You ask Dayo and Lydia to tell you more about booktalks.

They look at each other and nod in an understanding fashion before explaining how they view booktalks. Inspired recommendations. Purposeful. Sometimes infused with passion. Then Dayo says, "There's really no wrong way to do a booktalk."

Lydia adds, "Unless you give away the ending." They both laugh. You're taking mental notes and soaking up everything they share. Then she asks, "What's this?"

It's obviously a Swiss Army Knife, but that's not what she means. You respond, "Booktalks are the Swiss-Army knives of literacy leadership." You feel a little guilty for recycling the words your friend had shared moments ago without fully understanding their meaning.

Dayo does an enthusiastic drumroll on the table with the palms of his hands. It's enough to rattle the silverware. Clearly, he approves of the comparison. Your conversation starts to morph into an interactive game. "Tweezers!?" he says. Then he answers his own question by saying, "When you're doing a booktalk, you can pull out your favorite pictures and quotes!"

Lydia smiles and nods. This makes the competitor in you come alive and you shout, "Magnifying glass! Booktalks help you highlight important themes!" You do a less-than-subtle victory dance that ends with you looking through your hands as though they're magnifying glasses.

Dayo and Lydia burst out laughing. Lydia's purple-streaked hair is springing off her shoulders. She says, "Scissors!" Dayo looks at Lydia and raises an eyebrow. Lydia adds, "Start a booktalk with a personal connection or story. End it with a cliffhanger."

You visualize cutting off a booktalk before giving away the ending. It seems like a legit analogy. Dayo is staring intently at the utility tool and scrunching his nose. He says, "Toothpick thingy…" and then pauses. *This ought to be good.*

You've always wondered why utility knives have so many gadgets, but suddenly you're thankful they do.

- What is a book you would recommend to somebody you care about?
- What's another tool inside a utility knife that you could compare booktalks to?
- What are some unconventional ways we can recommend or connect readers to books they might enjoy?

"To promote wide reading outside the school day, students need recommendations."
(Marinak & Gambrell, 2016)

From Story to Practice

Readers should be allowed to interact socially without always having to write about what they're reading or fill in a log. They also need recommendations

FROM "THE 6 LITERACY LEVERS" BY BRAD GUSTAFSON (2021)

Figure 4.1: **Utility Knife Defined**

to continue reading. Booktalks support all this and more. Booktalks create connections by revealing new worlds and building bridges between readers and the books they haven't fallen in love with yet. Booktalks are the Swiss-Army knife of literacy leadership (see figure 4.2).

Suffice it to say, booktalks are a big deal. Admittedly, my kids would be the first to tell you I think a lot of things are a big deal. But that's mostly because I want to help them be successful. Here are a few more things on my big-deal list:

Manners are a big deal.
Integrity is a big deal.
Finding good-fit friends is a big deal.
Talking about books is a big deal.
Standing up for what's right is also a big deal.
Faith and Family are huge deals.

Figure 4.2: **The Swiss-Army Knife of Literacy Leadership**

My big-deal list makes a lot of sense to me now, but I haven't always held booktalks in the same high esteem as some of the other things on my big-deal list.

It's a distant memory now, but I remember walking into one of my kids' bedrooms to tuck her in on a nightly basis. Without fail, her big brown eyes would peer out from underneath the covers and a sleepy voice would say, *"Tell me about what you're reading, Daddy."*

It pains me to admit this, but sometimes I would dismiss those questions as bedtime-stall tactics. It took me a long time to realize how much she genuinely appreciated hearing about the different stories, characters, and authors I was reading. To this day, her eyes still light up when I tell her about the books I'm reading.

Booktalks shouldn't be limited to bedtime stories or nighttime tuck-ins. No matter what role you're serving in, recommending the books you love can strengthen relationships and enhance the other effective practices you're already doing. And that is a really big deal!

Key Drivers of Reading

Booktalks can be leveraged to improve the results you're achieving in areas that are already successful. Take the topic of book access for example—which is a key driver of reading and also a big deal. Access to books increases voluntary reading and has a positive impact on reading comprehension and students' motivation to read (Allington, 2014; Guthrie et al., 2006; Lindsay, 2013). Booktalks serve as a motivating bridge between the books students have access to and what they actually pick up and read.

Voluminous reading is another key driver and also a really big deal. Increased reading volume leads to increased reading achievement (Allington, 2014; Fisher & Frey, 2018). So, a reasonable question might be, *How do we increase the amount of time our students spend reading?* Simply telling students to read more is not the answer, but booktalks can be.

In fact, booktalks are such an important factor in increasing reading volume that Douglas Fisher and Nancy Frey (2018) identify booktalks as one of four crucial factors that increase voluntary independent reading outside of school. But the reasons, or *why*, behind sharing booktalks go beyond access and increasing the sheer number of books students are reading. Booktalks make a difference for all readers.

Why Share Booktalks?

Booktalks can fuel newfound motivation to read in students who have yet to discover their reading flow (Rodrigo et al., 2007). But they can also motivate voracious readers to branch out and read books they might not otherwise select on their own (Whittingham & Rickman, 2015). And because booktalks are inspired recommendations and not required reading, they offer students choice, which also increases their motivation to read (McClung et al., 2019).

Sharing the books we love is a force for good in the literacy world. Booktalks are like kryptonite to people who say they aren't readers yet! The best part is, anyone can do a booktalk. You don't need to hold a special license, lasso of truth, or Thor's hammer to talk about the books you love. And speaking of truth, the research is so compelling

> Sharing the books we love is a force for good in the literacy world. Booktalks are like kryptonite to people who say they aren't readers yet!

that everyone should be sharing them. Booktalks from trusted adults and peers fuel voluntary reading (Marinak & Gambrell, 2016).

No matter the role you're serving in, booktalks can support your leadership and work. They can be short and passion-infused recommendations presented before a meeting or professional development session. They could also span several minutes and be shared in a more conversational manner. A booktalk from a teacher to a group of students might start out sounding something like this:

"Yesterday in Social Studies, a few of you didn't believe me when I mentioned a former president swam with piranhas. But what if I told you that was only the beginning of the story? You won't believe all the twists and turns in *Death on the River of Doubt: Theodore Roosevelt's Amazon Adventure*. I've got a couple copies featured in our classroom library if you're up to it."

A booktalk from a teacher to a specific student might start out sounding something like this:

"I know you LOVE baseball and judging from the statistics you told me about last week, I have the perfect book for you. *Child of the Dream* was written by Jackie Robinson's daughter, Sharon

Robinson. It includes some super-cool information about her family and dad that you won't find anywhere else. Do you know what Jackie went on to do after his baseball career?"

A booktalk from a student to another student might sound something like this:

"I stayed up WAY too late last night reading. *Harry Potter and the Chamber of Secrets* is sooo good. You would love it, too."

As you can see, there are many ways to share a booktalk. The best booktalks I've heard haven't been perfect. They've been from the heart. It also helps to have a relationship with the person or people with whom you are sharing your booktalks. Just remember, booktalks don't have to be fancy, flashy, or a big production. And they are definitely not complete summaries. By their very definition, booktalks are recommendations (see figure 4.3).

A Word of Caution

Every reader responds differently to the opportunity to share. Forced sharing or making booktalks a mandatory public-speaking experience for all readers would be an inappropriate application of this lever.

I've noticed each of our three children respond very differently when asked about what they're reading. Our oldest daughter, Elise, prefers reading over almost anything. Literally. Reading is her safety net and solace in a world filled with people and complex social situations. Even when she's told to go outside and play, she'll often bring a book. You should never assume every student will be as excited to share a booktalk in the same manner. For as much as Elise loves reading, she would rather stop reading than talk about what she's reading. Forcing her to booktalk could potentially damage her relationship with books.

BOOKTALK

noun/verb /book-tawk/

1. An inspired recommendation.
2. Suggesting a book in the hope that somebody will love it as much as you do.

"The principal's booktalk was like kryptonite to colleagues who claimed they weren't really readers."

FROM "THE 6 LITERACY LEVERS" BY BRAD GUSTAFSON (2021)

Figure 4.3: **Booktalk Defined**

Anyone attempting to "help her" share a booktalk would need to be aware they are on very shaky ground.

In a similar vein, booktalks create culture, increase motivation, and support comprehension, but they shouldn't take the place of the explicit phonics instruction students need. You cannot create a culture of reading if you don't provide every student the reading instruction and responsive support they need.

How to Start a Booktalk

Most people have no problem telling others about a favorite movie or restaurant they enjoy. Unfortunately, telling others about the books you love isn't as common. Literacy leaders create a culture where book-talking is as natural and worthy of our time as the conversations we have about other things we love. I'm going to share a few strategies to help.

There's no right or wrong way to start a booktalk. However, it is helpful to start with something that piques the interest of potential readers. I refer to this approach as using a hook. Hooks need not be fancy or polished and there are zillions from which to choose. The list below features 26 examples arranged alphabetically from A to Z (see figure 4.4).

BOOKTALK A TO Z HOOKS

ASK A QUESTION
BE HONEST ABOUT WHY YOU LAUGHED, CRIED, ETC.
CONNECT THE BOOK TO ANOTHER PERSON'S PASSIONS
DO AN IMPERSONATION
EXPLAIN WHY THE PROTAGONIST SHOULD WIN AN AWARD
FIND A SURPRISING FACT
GIVE AN EXAMPLE OF A POSITIVE LEADERSHIP TRAIT
HOLD UP YOUR FAVORITE PAGE OR PICTURE
"IF YOU LIKE ____ YOU'LL LOVE THIS BOOK!"
JUSTIFY WHY AN ALTERNATE TITLE WOULD BE BETTER
KEEP A TIMER ON AND TRY TO DO YOUR BOOKTALK IN 30 SECONDS!
LET SOMEBODY KNOW WHY THIS IS THE PERFECT BOOK FOR THEM
MAKE IT A MOVIE...WHO WOULD PLAY THE LEADING ROLE?
NOTICE SOMETHING ABOUT THE BOOK NOBODY ELSE HAS
OPEN WITH A SOUND EFFECT FROM THE BOOK
PICK A PARTNER AND THEN DIALOGUE ABOUT THE BOOK
QUIETLY SUMMARIZE THE SCARIEST PART TO BUILD SUSPENSE
READ A POWERFUL QUOTE
SHARE A CONNECTION YOU HAVE WITH THE AUTHOR
TRY TO INVENT (OR BUILD) SOMETHING RELATED TO THE TEXT
USE A PROP
VINDICATE THE ANTAGONIST!
WEAR A COSTUME
X-RAY INTO THE AUTHOR'S MIND. WHY DOES THIS BOOK MATTER?
"YOU HAVE TO READ THIS BECAUSE..."
ZZZ.... (EXPLAIN WHY THIS IS THE BOOK OF YOUR DREAMS!)

"BOOKTALKS ARE THE SWISS-ARMY KNIFE OF LITERACY LEADERSHIP"

FROM "THE 6 LITERACY LEVERS" BY BRAD GUSTAFSON (2021)

Figure 4.4: **Booktalk Hooks A to Z**

If you're sharing at a school assembly, you might want a prop or picture to help everyone engage. If you're celebrating a few new titles being added to a classroom library, you could try keeping a timer going and challenge yourself to booktalk each title in thirty seconds or less. If you're connecting individually with a student or colleague, you might give an example of a positive leadership trait within the book and make a personal connection to the other person. With slight adjustments, you can make any hook work for you.

For example, the booktalk hook for the letter E (Explain why the protagonist should win an award) could be adopted so readers design an award for a book they enjoy (see figure 4.5). One of the benefits of using hooks is that they can feel more concrete than just telling a person to start talking about a book. Giving readers the option to talk about an award they created in a smaller setting or writing a reflection would be another way to honor different preferences and needs.

Figure 4.5: **Build-Your-Own Book Award**

Creating Booktalk Hooks

Whether you've been recommending books for a long time or you're relatively new to booktalking, practicing new strategies builds an important fluency. For this activity, think about a book you recently read or love. The goal will be to try and think of several different hooks for the same book. I created a template using only the vowels from the original A to Z list I shared previously (see figure 4.6).

1. Start by choosing a book you really enjoy or one you recently read. Write the title of the book in the shaded section at the bottom of the template.

CH. 4 ACTIVITY 1	**PRACTICE BUILDING BOOKTALK HOOKS**
A	Ask a question
E	Explain why the protagonist should win an award
I	"If you like _____ you'll love this book"
O	Open up with a sound effect
U	Use a prop
Y	"You have to read this because…"
TITLE:	

FROM "THE 6 LITERACY LEVERS" BY BRAD GUSTAFSON (2021)

Figure 4.6: **Booktalk Hooks (Activity)**

2. Next, read through the prompts and circle the vowels you'd like to try to create booktalk hooks for. Not all the hooks will work with every book, but it can be good practice (and a fun challenge) to try to create different hooks for the same book.

3. Feel free to reference the examples below if you'd like additional explanation for any of the prompts. I created the sample hooks for the book, *Spruce and Lucy* by my good friend Todd Nesloney.

   · *A: Ask a question.*
   Have you ever felt alone? Have you ever compared yourself to others and felt as though you weren't enough? Something tells me you might be inspired by the main character in this book, Spruce...

   · E: Explain why the Protagonist should win an award.
   Ahem. (Using announcer voice.) The nominees for the "Better Together" award are *Spruce* and *Lucy*. In this book, the two unlikely friends show courage and vulnerability by reaching out, opening up, and persevering together.

   · I: "If you like _____ you'll love this book."
   If you like *The Giving Tree*, you'll love *Spruce and Lucy* by Todd Nesloney. *Spruce and Lucy* puts a modern-day spin on the theme of friendship using relatable characters and an inspiring message of hope.

   · O: Open with a sound effect from the book.
   "Sniff, sniff, WAAAHHHH!" Spruce felt defeated, inadequate, and all alone. But this isn't a story of sadness; it's a story about friendship and doing great things.

   · *U: Use a prop.*
   [Hold up a small twig or branch with one or two leaves remaining.]

   · *Y: You have to read this because...* You have to read *Spruce and Lucy* because it teaches kids that being small doesn't mean they can't do big things. And it does so in an incredibly heartwarming way!

4. Build a hook for each vowel you selected. This activity is even more fun when two people who read the same book create and compare hooks together.

5. Last, share your hook with somebody you think might enjoy the book you selected.

The most effective way to create a culture of booktalking is to actually start booktalking. Hooks can help you start. It only takes a few seconds to share a short hook before a meeting, school assembly, professional development session, or during transition times with students.

By making booktalking part of the cadence of your classroom and school, you create the conditions where sharing the books people love is as likely as having a passion-infused conversation about your favorite foods or movies.

Bring the Booktalk H.E.A.T.

Most people understand how powerful a recommendation from a friend or co-worker can be. Even anonymous reviews carry some weight—look no further than your favorite online retailer to see how ratings and reviews influence decision making. By being more purposeful in how you teach the skill of booktalking, you increase the capacity of readers to influence culture.

There's no right or wrong way to do a booktalk, but some booktalks are more effective than others. The H.E.A.T. acronym is a framework that will help you and your students become more skilled in sharing the books you love—which translates into more people wanting to read the books you're recommending (see figure 4.7).

Booktalk H.E.A.T. breaks down booktalks into four important parts. Each of the parts can be practiced and improved, so the model is

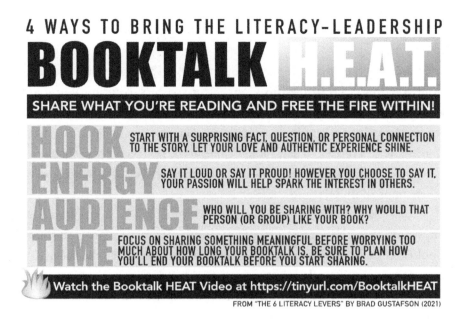

Figure 4.7: **Booktalk H.E.A.T.**

an effective learning tool for all ages. (You'll notice a video URL listed at the bottom of the Booktalk H.E.A.T. graphic. If you're looking for a quick tutorial, you may want to check that out.)

The opening **Hook** engages potential readers by starting with something interesting, heartfelt, and worthy of their attention. Introducing yourself and regurgitating the title of a book are not the most effective ways to hook potential readers in. (You can always introduce yourself and share a book's title and author after sharing a hook.)

Your **Energy** level matters. Think about the tone you hope to convey and plan your content accordingly. Speak with confidence and exude a passion for the book you're recommending. If you're not excited about your book, other people probably won't be either. If you're doing your booktalk on video, I always suggest upping the energy level and volume of your voice slightly. This tends to compensate for the different type of connection people experience via video. If you're too quiet, regardless of whether it's in-person or on video, it can be challenging for people to engage.

Knowing your **Audience** is helpful. As I've mentioned several times, reading is a relationship. Connection matters. Anytime you share a book recommendation, it's important for the people you're with to see how much you genuinely care about *them*, not just the book you're sharing. If you're able to say, *I know some of the things you care about and I really think this book will be one of them*, it shows your audience you've taken steps to understand their needs.

The specific amount of **Time** you spend on a booktalk is less important than the connection and meaning you create when you share. Booktalks can be any length. Oftentimes, the sweet spot is between 1-2 minutes long, although I've been known to challenge myself by sharing booktalks in 30-second bursts. If you're sharing a booktalk over a public-address system as part of morning announcements or during halftime at a school sporting event, it's probably best to err on the side of brevity. However, if you're sharing with a smaller group, and have fewer time constraints, your booktalk could be five or more minutes long and still be meaningful.

My best advice is to practice how you're going to end your booktalk. I've found that most people struggle with finding a succinct way to wind down their booktalk. If you want to practice your timing, start there. You're more likely to meander if you don't plan how you'll finish your booktalk. You might consider connecting your ending to your opening hook. Or you could conclude by saying something simple like, "I really think you'll love this book."

Planning Your First Leadership Booktalk

Modeling your learning and the struggles you encounter along the way is one of the most powerful things you can do as a leader. Using the

H.E.A.T. framework will help you plan a booktalk you can share with your colleagues, class, or school. This activity uses a leadership book-talk template to help you plan your approach (see figure 4.8).

The template has enough space to jot down a few notes that will serve as reminders to yourself later. It is not intended to be used as a script. The goal is to think through what you want to share and then speak from the heart when you're eventually sharing your booktalk.

1. Think about a book you'd like to recommend to others.
2. Create a hook. In my experience, the best hooks are the ones you're excited to share. One of my favorite hooks has always been sharing a personal story or connection because I don't have to work too hard at trying to remember my own authentic experiences.
3. Make a note of the energy you want to convey and plan your content accordingly. Consider tapping into the theme or tone

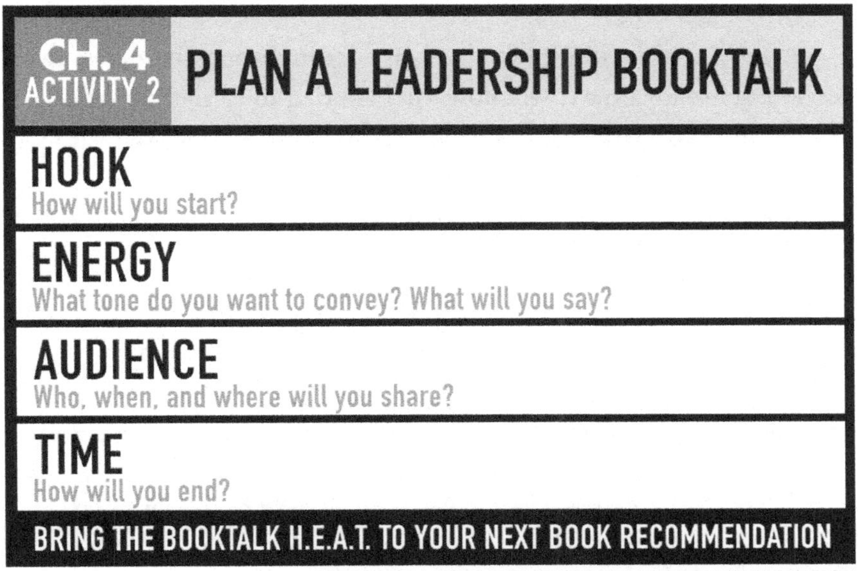

CH. 4 ACTIVITY 2 PLAN A LEADERSHIP BOOKTALK

HOOK
How will you start?

ENERGY
What tone do you want to convey? What will you say?

AUDIENCE
Who, when, and where will you share?

TIME
How will you end?

BRING THE BOOKTALK H.E.A.T. TO YOUR NEXT BOOK RECOMMENDATION

FROM "THE 6 LITERACY LEVERS" BY BRAD GUSTAFSON (2021)

Figure 4.8: **Plan a Leadership Booktalk (Activity)**

of the book itself. If the book is intended to inspire, you may wish to choose a few uplifting quotes to share. If the book is a mystery, your booktalk may be more mysterious and could end on a cliffhanger.

4. Identify your audience. Think about the specific people you plan to share your booktalk with or the specific place or meeting at which you will lead the booktalk. Some possible audiences include a classroom, school assembly, morning announcement, PTA/PTO meeting, staff meeting, parent night, or video that's posted to a school social media channel. Write down with whom, when, and where you will share your booktalk, then be sure to follow through.

5. Reflect upon how much time you want to share. To help you keep within the window of time you want to share, plan your final sentence or conclusion, and write that down. Deciding on a crisp ending will leave a powerful last impression.

After you have your booktalk planned, run through it once or twice to get a sense for how it will flow. As I alluded to earlier, the goal is to speak from the heart. The goal is *not* perfection. Holding yourself to an impossible standard is the quickest way to ensure your booktalk fails. Besides that, people tend to appreciate when leaders exhibit vulnerability by trying new things.

Ideas You Can Implement

Steven Geis is a principal in Minnesota. Dr. Geis has been a strong champion for literacy for as long as I've known him, but it's the consistent manner in which he shares booktalks that I find really inspiring. He even managed to add a heartfelt booktalk into his introductory remarks at a National Association of Elementary Principals conference while he was serving as president. By sharing a book at the beginning of every meeting, he creates a buzz and anticipation before meetings.

Dr. Geis has shown us that booktalks should not be limited to literacy meetings. Whether you're facilitating a training on a math curriculum, kicking off a weekly staff meeting, or planning district-level professional development, you can start with a booktalk. If you do this consistently, some people might even secretly look forward to hearing about whatever book you plan to share—which could eventually lead to inviting others to share.

Another idea that can be seamlessly integrated into work that's already being done is to ask candidates to share a booktalk during interviews (see figure 4.9). If you want to create a culture of literacy, it helps to hire readers. Asking candidates to talk about books also serves as a visible reminder of your school values and compass to the hiring team.

What you give time to is what you love. You can start to change culture simply by establishing the expectation that potential employees talk about their reading lives before they join the team.

INTERVIEW QUESTION

"BOOKTALKS" ARE THE READER'S EQUIVALENT TO TELLING SOMEBODY ABOUT A MUST-SEE MOVIE OR TALKING ABOUT A RESTAURANT YOU REALLY ENJOY.

CAN YOU PLEASE SHARE A BOOKTALK FOR US SO WE CAN HEAR ABOUT A BOOK YOU MIGHT RECOMMEND TO A STUDENT OR COLLEAGUE?

LOOK FORS: INDICATION OF A READING LIFE, WILLINGNESS TO BOOKTALK, AND REASON A TITLE WAS SHARED.

FROM "THE 6 LITERACY LEVERS" BY BRAD GUSTAFSON (2021)

Figure 4.9: **Sample Interview Question**

Whether you're asking interview questions or sharing short book-talks before meetings, being mindful of the different ways people prefer to process and share is important. At the same time, it's important to consider new techniques and platforms students are using to connect, learn, and express themselves.

Several years ago, I saw a hashtag on Twitter (#6WordBooktalk) that contained booktalks that were only six words long. I immediately thought the six-word concept could be a good entry point for readers of all ages to try booktalking regardless of whether they are posted to social media. The activity can easily be adopted so it's inclusive of people who prefer writing over recording themselves on video.

A six-word booktalk is as simple as the name implies, but don't let the brevity of the final product fool you. Sometimes we make the mistake of thinking that *succinct* is the same as *simple*. However, something can be short and still be complex and insightful. Finding a way to pack the most important parts of a book's plot into six words is not easy. Here is an example of a #6WordBooktalk for *Dry* by Neal Shusterman and Jarrod Shusterman as an example (see figure 4.10). I'm not sure if the six words I chose do the book justice, but be sure to read it for yourself because it is a fantastic book.

I've also seen readers create flyers using the #6WordBooktalk concept (see figure 4.11). The tear-off flyer approach provides students an authentic purpose for sharing because other readers can interact with the flyers. Of course, students can be invited to share why they selected their six words to ensure the project doesn't cut off important conversations.

Six-word booktalks are ripe for collaboration beyond the walls of your classroom and school. Sharing booktalks on social media provides literacy leaders a unique opportunity to interact with a larger community of readers.

I'm cognizant of the fact that many educators are less active on social media and some have chosen to avoid social media altogether. I

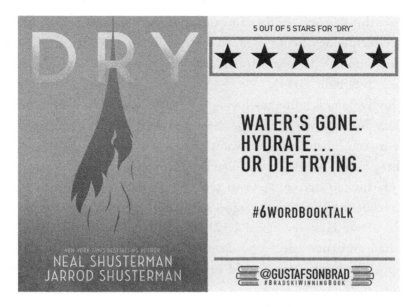

Figure 4.10: **#6WordBooktalk**

Figure 4.11: **Booktalk Flyers**

respect this decision. At the same time, I hope students have the chance to see technology being used to connect in safe and authentic ways during school. When this doesn't happen, they can become frustrated (Dietrich & Balli, 2014).

Joy DeJong is a literacy-loving teacher in Iowa. She shared a Seven-Day Book Cover Challenge she's used with students to help them have more authentic conversations about what they're reading. (The hashtag for the activity was #7DayBookCoverChallenge.)

Joy invited her students to start by designing a name card as a header for the book cover images they would display over the course of the seven days (see figure 4.12). On the first day of the challenge, she had students select one cover they wanted to display for any reason. The book covers could be images printed from online, dust jackets, or the actual book. Cover selections couldn't be accompanied by any words. Students repeated the process for seven days without providing any explanation for the books they added to their individual displays.

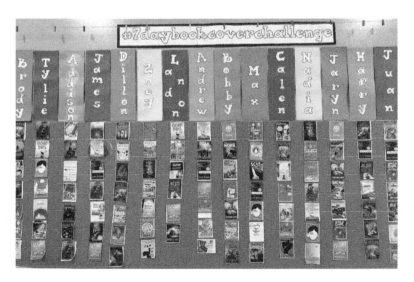

Figure 4.12: **Seven-Day Book Cover Challenge**

On the final day, students were invited to ask questions and share. As you can probably imagine, conversations on the final day erupted like a can of soda that had been shaken before being opened!

Like all ideas, this one provides an opportunity for literacy leaders to apply multiple levers. In addition to the utility knife, my mind goes to the value of the walking stick. Asking questions that ensure an activity like this is accessible and inclusive to each reader is important.

Many of us serve students who haven't fully developed their conversational skills yet, whether from lack of practice or limited proficiency with English. Pre-teaching how to construct conversation sequences for authentic experiences will strengthen their skills and ability to enter the world of booktalks more successfully (Waedaoh & Sinwongsuwat, 2018). An example of a conversation sequence to initiate with a classmate for this activity might be something like:

- "I noticed you chose the cover for the book [say title]. Can you tell me why you selected it?
  [Listen to classmate's response]
- "Is there a character or part of the book you think I might enjoy?"
  [Listen to classmate's response]
- "Thanks for sharing with me."

Regardless of the ideas you and your team decide to try, I encourage you to remember that booktalks do not need to be fancy or a big production. One year, our school started a student-video series called *Bookcast*. It was one of the least scripted and organic projects we've tried. I basically ate lunch with a different group of students each week and we'd hit "record" as we talked about books, laughed, and learned together. Bookcast was low-prep for me and highly motivating for readers. But it was also different, which made me uncomfortable at times.

I tend to over plan and can struggle with free-flowing videos. This alone would've been reason enough for us not to try Bookcast. However, my friend George Couros once said something that really stuck with me. I don't even recall the topic being discussed, but I do remember how he approached it. Instead of limiting conversations and planning in a manner that only addresses the worst things that could happen, he also asked, "What's the best thing that could happen?" This is an important question to carry with you as you practice using the utility knife and introducing its versatility to others. Because booktalks are a big deal.

Questions to Push the Field Forward

+ What are some ways you can empower and engage all staff in modeling booktalks and other meaningful conversations about reading?
+ How will you keep booktalks authentic and not turn them into yet another assignment or "string" a school ties to the reading lives of students?

Leverage Your Literacy Leadership Schoolwide

Booktalks take many forms and are truly the Swiss-Army knife of literacy leadership, from pre-planned booktalks to organic discussions about what you're reading. I've visited classrooms where teachers have an informal sign-up list scrawled on the whiteboard. Students interested in sharing a short booktalk during transition time simply add their name to the list with no strings attached.

Challenge yourself to start small and model booktalking. Then, invite others into the fold by having a conversation about how booktalking might be something you and your team leverage collectively. Try to think about how booktalks might enhance the work and traditions you're already committed to before inventing new work for yourselves (see figure 4.13).

Maybe it's a series of super-short booktalks shared at halftime of a big game. It could be asking new hires to share their favorite book as part of how they're introduced to the broader school community.

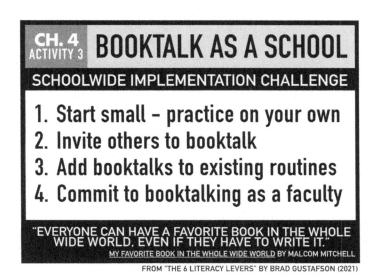

Figure 4.13: **Schoolwide Implementation Challenge**

Maybe it's just agreeing to start every meeting with a heartfelt recommendation. Something short, meaningful, and authentic. Or maybe it's making a commitment as an entire staff to share one booktalk with students over the next several weeks that somehow relates to your content area or a pastime you enjoy.

I'm imagining a middle-school math teacher booktalking *Titans* by Victoria Scott and celebrating how the main character, Astrid, uses her mathematical prowess to compete in a high-tech horse racing circuit. Or a high-school foreign language teacher highlighting how culture and language is woven into *On the Hook* by Francisco X. Stork in the most beautiful ways. Or an elementary school science or special education teacher booktalking *Forget Me Not* by Ellie Terry because the main character's identity is forged from a love of science (and many other things) that are above and beyond the disability she has.

The possibilities, books, and content areas are endless. Imagine the culture you and your team can create by trying something different together.

CHAPTER 5

The Catapult

I magine this: A waiter stops by your table to ask if you need any-thing, but you don't feel as though you need another thing in the entire world. The moment you just shared with Dayo and Lydia was electric. The utility-knife brainstorming. The laughter. The connection.

Dayo looks up. You notice him bite his tongue for a split second before he looks towards Lydia. He turns to you and says, "You have got to join our book club." Maybe it's the way he emphasizes the words, "book club," but you immediately sense this is a club you want to be in.

You look at Lydia half expecting her to object, but she does just the opposite. Her eyebrows are raised with anticipation. You're about to ask her how the book club works when you hear a commotion coming from across the restaurant. The next thing you see is your literacy men-tor lugging something towards your table. Something big.

You feel your eyes blinking as though they're still trying to process the spectacle, but this doesn't change the fact you're staring at a giant catapult. "What the...?"

Now your literacy mentor is standing next to the contraption while smiling at Lydia and Dayo. "It appears as though I didn't need to bring this," she says.

"You think?!" you say with eyes wide open. You had been wondering where she was, but this explains a lot.

"I wanted to share one more thing with you. Something important before our meeting is over," she says as she motions towards the catapult.

You're laughing now, but you're also dying to know how something so large could even fit through the front doors of the restaurant. Or why it's sitting next to your table. You look towards Dayo and Lydia, but they're so calm they may as well have been the ones who helped lug in the antique contraption. You start to ask, "Wh…?"

As the word forms on your lips, your mentor starts nodding with intentionality and says, "I bring this everywhere." The reassuring smile on her face somehow convinces you this is true. It's also the kind of smile that says, *You can ask me anything* and actually means it.

Over the course of the evening you learn that the thing you dismissed as an *antique* is actually *timeless*. With the help of Dayo and Lydia, your mentor explains how the catapult represents connection. More specifically, it represents the role that relationships, connection, and community play in creating a culture of reading and a community of readers.

Before the night is over, you think the catapult is the thing you might need most to move forward on your literacy leadership journey. Without the catapult, things like the compass, authentic invitations, walking stick, and utility knife are less meaningful. Relationships inspire trust. Connection changes the game. Together, they move a reading community forward.

It seems to happen too fast, but just as quickly as your mystery meeting started, the evening ends. As Dayo, Lydia, and your mentor transition towards the door, a laugh that's a little louder than you intended escapes. Shaking your head in disbelief at what you're about to do, you study the path from your table to the exit and start pulling. It turns out the catapult is lighter than it looks.

- What are some of the specific things you do as a literacy leader to build *relationships* with and between readers?
- How might a person know if they are part of a reading *community*?
- What books, characters, and authors have you experienced a *connection* with?

Figure 5.1: **The Catapult Defined**

"Connection is the energy that is created between people when they feel seen, heard, and valued— when they can give and receive without judgement."
~Brené Brown

From Story to Practice

Just like a catapult converts stored energy into motion, connection propels culture forward. You can't create enriched reading experiences without connection. Connection is relationships. It is a community of readers. And it is the palpable energy we feel between the books, characters, genres, and people we love. Connection can be invisible or outwardly apparent, but it is always important.

Literacy leaders can leverage the catapult in a multitude of ways, many of which work in tandem with the other levers we've explored already. For example:

+ We champion community when we work with others to co-create a *compass*. Channeling energy into a shared vision serves all students.
+ We create a sense of belonging when the *invitation* includes everyone. Recognizing the strengths of others increases individual and collective ownership.
+ We build trust when we carry a *walking stick* consistently over time. Asking questions with curiosity enhances a community's ability to confront potentially damaging practices.
+ We grow culture when we model new and meaningful ways to use the *utility knife*. Sharing the books we love in an authentic manner sends positive ripples into the reading universe.

Connection is the lever that strengthens all the other levers. Relationships strengthen a person's resolve just as commitment inspires action.

The Power of Connection

One of my most memorable professional development moments happened when I was with a small group of friends at a national principals' conference. It just so happens that the friends I was with were also avid readers. We were sitting in the middle of a massive conference center filled with thousands of people. Right before the final speaker took the stage, one of my friends noticed a few open seats towards the front.

The closing speaker was the New York Times bestselling author and Newbery Medal winner, Kwame Alexander, so seeing empty seats up front felt like a mirage. It also meant we had to go check them out. We were pleased with our decision until we made it up front and realized why the seats were empty. They had been roped off for V.I.P.s and the conference organizers.

As the keynote kicked off, a sense of panic set in. However, my literacy-loving friends and I couldn't fathom a world in which any seat would remain empty at the front of a Kwame Alexander keynote. We stealthily ducked under the rope and claimed the second-row seats. Needless to say, Kwame's keynote was nothing short of incredible. The energy. Stories. And poetry. I could feel every syllable he was speaking (see figure 5.2). Experiencing it all alongside the people who I considered a big part of my reading life meant a lot.

Figure 5.2: **V.I.P. Kwame Seats**

After the keynote, the conference emcees took the stage and announced that Kwame would be signing books in the bookstore. That's when my friends and I realized we had a new problem. We were so close to the stage that there were now thousands of conference attendees who were standing between us and where the book signing would take place.

Without hesitation, I threw the strap of my work bag over my shoulder. We looked to our left and then to our right to calculate the least disruptive path out. Avoiding the coffee cups, knees, and personal effects of everyone else was an impossible task. As I approached the aisle and stanchion rope, I ducked down and tried to crawl past the barrier. Except there was one problem: I was stuck.

No matter how hard I leaned forward I couldn't move. My arms were on the floor supporting my body weight while I was simultaneously cradling my work bag. To make matters worse, I had managed to squeeze far enough past the person at the end of the row that my head was sticking out into the aisle for everyone behind us to see.

I could literally see my escape path but couldn't find a way to free myself. After the longest minute of my life, the friend who had been crawling behind me realized what the problem was. The strap from my work bag had somehow snagged the last chair in the row in front of ours right before I had ducked under the rope. My friend helped unhook my bag and we took the walk of shame out of the conference room.

By that time, a long line had formed in front of us. But we made the most of it. In between laughs, my friends and I took turns telling and retelling what had just happened from our different vantage points. As we listened to each other share, you could almost feel an unspoken bond, a connection and energy readers feel when they're with other readers.

A reading community doesn't just read together. They laugh. Share stories. Reflect. And find ways to catapult across large crowds of people to get closer to authors. The same sense of connection that propelled a few literacy-loving friends and me across a conference center can be nurtured in your school. It's not something that usually happens overnight. Or with great fanfare. But when it happens, you can feel it. As literacy leaders, we would do well to co-create a reading community.

A reading community is co-created by countless individuals who contribute in different ways (see figure 5.3), working to create the conditions in which every reader in the community thrives, but also partnering to create shared experiences that bring everyone together. The work any one person or leader in a community does may seem insignificant, but the ideas, investments, and relationship building works together to create something special.

Creating a reading community takes intentionality and time. You don't just speak a community into existence or proclaim you have one.

Figure 5.3: **Reading Community Defined**

Here is a list of things that will help you build relationships and create connection so that the reading community you're co-creating can thrive (see figure 5.4). The list is by no means exhaustive, but it does contain several strategies you can do from wherever you're leading.

15 WAYS TO CO-CREATE A READING COMMUNITY

1. FOCUS LESS ON FLASH AND MORE ON MEANINGFUL READING EXPERIENCES
2. GUSH ABOUT YOUR FAVORITE BOOKS AND AUTHORS
3. PROVIDE INSTRUCTION AND SUPPORTS THAT ENSURE ALL STUDENTS LEARN HOW TO READ
4. CHAMPION CHOICE AND PROVIDE SUPPORT DURING DAILY INDEPENDENT READING TIME
5. ENSURE ALL READERS FEEL SEEN AND SUPPORTED
6. ASK QUESTIONS THAT ILLUMINATE THE READING LIVES OF APPLICANTS DURING INTERVIEWS
7. INJECT LITERACY INTO EXISTING EVENTS
8. INVITE AUTHORS IN AND TREAT THEM LIKE CELEBRITIES
9. PLAN OPPORTUNITIES FOR FAMILIES TO CONNECT AROUND READING THROUGHOUT THE YEAR
10. BUILD A BUDGET THAT PRIORITIZES THE SCHOOL MEDIA PROGRAM AND CLASSROOM LIBRARIES
11. DESIGN AN ENVIRONMENT THAT CELEBRATES READING
12. ACTIVELY SHARE YOUR READING LIFE WITH OTHERS
13. CREATE ADDITIONAL CONNECTION USING TOOLS THAT ARE RELEVANT TO READERS
14. BOOKTALK, BOOKTALK, BOOKTALK!
15. CELEBRATE STUDENTS' INTERESTS AND CULTURE

FROM "THE 6 LITERACY LEVERS" BY BRAD GUSTAFSON (2021)

Figure 5.4: **15 Ways to Co-create a Reading Community**

Ideas You Can Implement

The ideas that follow come from literacy leaders serving at several different levels of leadership, formal and informal. The ideas are not intended to be checklist items that you take-and-bake in your school. You will want to work with your team to determine what might be meaningful to your community. To make things easier to come back to later, I've numbered the ideas below, so they correspond with the list of fifteen ways to co-create a reading community:

1. Focus Less on Flash and More on Meaningful Reading Experiences.
    Sometimes the most important work being done is the most difficult for others to see. Lindsey Sullivan is a 5th grade teacher and literacy leader in Wayzata Public Schools. Her work with creating a community of readers is incredible. Lindsey wants students to think deeply about what they're reading and be able to have authentic conversations connected to their thoughts. She uses an interactive reading protocol to help with these goals (see figure 5.5). Over the years, she's noticed the protocol also helps students build trust and form friendships.
    The protocols Lindsey has landed on are not necessarily the point here, although we're sharing them in case it's helpful. The point is, the meaningful literacy leadership work Lindsey is doing to build relationships is not flashy. But it creates connection and that is leading to the creation of a special community of readers. I've had the chance to observe some of the deep and organic conversations that take place in this community and am floored every single time.

2. Gush About Your Favorite Books and Authors
    Passion is contagious and I haven't met too many people more passionate about books than John Schu. Whether he's gushing about his favorite books during school visits or connecting with authors on social media (@MrSchuReads), it's impossible to walk away from an

INTERACTIVE READING PROTOCOL
USED BY A 5TH-GRADE TEACHER TO BUILD A READING COMMUNITY

- STUDENTS KEEP THEIR READER'S NOTEBOOKS OPEN DURING READ ALOUD TIME
- TEACHER OCCASIONALLY STOPS READING TO POSE AN OPEN-ENDED QUESTION
- TEACHER PROVIDES A FEW MINUTES OF PROTECTED THINKING/WRITING TIME
- STUDENTS QUIETLY RESPOND TO THE OPEN-ENDED QUESTION IN THEIR READER'S NOTEBOOK WHILE BEING SURE TO JUSTIFY THEIR THINKING
- TEACHER PROMPTS STUDENTS TO TALK THROUGH THEIR THOUGHTS WITH THEIR TABLE OR ONE-ON-ONE WITH A PARTNER
- TEACHER OPENS UP THE CONVERSATIONS TO THE WHOLE CLASS AND CALLS ON 2-3 STUDENTS...OR INVITES ONE PERSON FROM EACH TABLE TO SHARE
- TEACHER MODELS WHAT IT LOOKS AND SOUNDS LIKE TO BUILD ON THE IDEAS OF OTHERS, PUSH BACK, OR PROBE FOR MORE INFORMATION
- TEACHER CONTINUES THE READ ALOUD AND OCCASIONALLY WEAVES IN THE PROTOCOLS ABOVE WHILE BEING CAREFUL TO MAINTAIN A READING FLOW

FROM "THE 6 LITERACY LEVERS" BY BRAD GUSTAFSON (2021)

Figure 5.5: **Interactive Read Aloud Protocol**

encounter with John without feeling viscerally connected—to him as well as a broader community of readers.

Just writing about all the times I've seen John share this passion makes me smile. Like when he's describing the scent of new books,

> The energy you show up with can catapult people to positive places long after you leave the room.

doing dust jacket reveals, and sharing Kate Dicamillo stories. The energy you show up with can catapult people to positive places long after you leave the room.

3. Provide Instruction and Supports that Ensure All Students Learn to Read

You cannot co-create a reading community that serves all students without creating systems to help everyone learn to read. Don Vu is the author of *Life, Literacy, and the Pursuit of Happiness*, a book about supporting immigrant and refugee children through the power of reading.

When Don was a principal at Barrett Ranch Elementary School in California, half the students in his school were learning English as a second language. While Don and his team were doing many things to create a culture of reading, they knew they needed to ensure all students had the skills to fully participate in the reading community.

Learning to read requires explicit instruction over time; it doesn't happen naturally, through osmosis, or even by being immersed in a print-rich environment (International Dyslexia Association, 2018). To move forward on the mission of empowering all students with the skills needed to read, Don's school committed to using a consistent approach. This included common materials and assessments when teaching students to learn how to read. Professional Learning Communities (PLCs) met weekly and focused on students' progress in English language arts. Don's staff would spend time going over students' progress and needs every trimester which is one reason why the common assessments were helpful.

Phonics, phonological awareness, sight words, etc. played a critical role in reading instruction. They also used flexible grouping to remain responsive to students' needs and ever-changing language skills. Depending on the grade level and need, teachers spent 30-45 minutes a day working on foundational reading skills. If a student did not respond to that focused and intensive instruction, there were other supports and interventions available.

Don's school became really good at teaching students how to read, but they started to notice a different problem. Students weren't enjoying it. The impact on English learners and students in special education programs was worse, as they were getting a double dose of the phonics regimen.

Don and his school knew they needed to continue developing the *skill* of reading, but they started to focus on developing the *will* to read as well. To help make reading fun again (for teachers, too), they launched a "Broncos Read" campaign that was based upon their school mascot. The connection between *being able* to read and *wanting* to read has been restored—and their community is stronger because of it.

4. Champion Choice and Provide Support during Daily Independent Reading Time

Despite four decades of research showing the importance of independent reading time, most schools still struggle to provide all students daily independent reading time (Harvey & Ward, 2017). In a 2018 Literacy Leadership Research Brief from the International Literacy Association, only 17% of students ages 6-17 reported reading independently during the school day.

I posed this problem of practice on social media to learn how other literacy leaders are trying to make daily independent reading a priority for all readers. Since this chapter focuses on relationships, connection, and community, I thought you might appreciate hearing how some of the literacy leaders I've connected with are trying to navigate this complex issue.

+ Rachel Greengold (@rachelgreengold) is a 4th grade teacher in Texas. All her students get daily independent reading time during the first twenty minutes of class each day. Students are not pulled for other services or support during this time.
+ Dr. Justin S. Grigg (@JGrigg_LCPS) is a director of elementary education in Virginia. His district built independent reading time into the ELA block. They also added book nooks in hallways and created a space in the lunchroom called "The Literacy Cafe" for students wanting to read during lunch. By increasing access to high-interest books and creating protected time and

spaces to read, more students are reading during the school day.

- Joan Bryant (@JoanBryant6) is starting her 24th year as an educator in Virginia. She's taught Head Start, Kindergarten, 1st, and 3rd grade classes and has always tried to build independent reading time into her language arts blocks. However, she believes students are best served when administrators partner with teachers on problems of practice. Saving a seat at the table for teachers to talk through ideas and issues increases the likelihood of success.

- Stephen Grenham (@s_grenham) is a principal in Massachusetts. His school treats independent reading and choice as a non-negotiable. To get to this point, an ELA team consisting of two teachers from each grade level worked with their reading specialists to determine what they wanted out of ELA time. This process involved in-house professional development and research. Focused feedback and support are now being provided to different students during independent reading time each day. They also have a "What I Need" time (a.k.a. WIN time) set aside so students who need to be pulled out for music lessons, reading/math support, guidance, etc. are less likely to miss independent reading time. The WIN block can also be used for reading support and check-ins with students.

- Teresa Corrigan (@TeresaCorrigan2) is a retired first grade teacher who is now at the college level in New York. She suggested re-looking at classroom schedules to create non-negotiable reading times during which teachers could also circulate the room and confer with students. For example, by providing time for students to complete math work first thing in the morning as they arrive, it might be possible to shave a few minutes from the math block. Looking at the schedule more holistically might make it possible to put together a chunk of protected independent reading time with accompanying support.

+ Dr. Peter Carpenter (@drpcarpenter) is a personalized learning and leadership development supervisor in Maryland.
When he was serving as a principal, his team tried to use a
"both-and" approach instead of an "either-or" mentality. Their
goal was to get every child on grade-level by the end of 2nd
grade *and* loving to read. To do this, his leadership team looked
at the schedule and decided to take five minutes from each of
the major subject areas to create a 35-minute block of time for
interventions and enrichment. This helped protect the ELA
block from pull-outs and ensured all students received the
phonics instruction, comprehension/reading skills, and independent reading practice.

+ Beth Jarzabek (@bethiej1027) is a middle school teacher in
Massachusetts. She shared how her school administration prioritizes reading by scheduling a schoolwide time during which
everybody stops what they're doing to read for fifteen minutes
each day.

+ Jonathan Winkle (@Mr_Jon_Winkle) is a principal in Pennsyl-
vania. He shared that his school created a separate intervention
and enrichment block to minimize students being pulled for
services during independent reading time. Independent reading
was kept within the core ELA block.

+ Danielle Brkich (@77techdb) is an ELA Teacher and Technology Coach in Ohio. She reminded me that we do not need to
schedule independent reading at the exact same time for all students. It's possible to build additional flexibility into the schedule by using asynchronous activities and screencasts to support
small group instruction. This flexibility can help educators
provide all students protected reading time, even if it's done in
smaller groups or rotations.

+ Jay Clark is a superintendent in Ohio. When he was a middle
school principal, his team was noticing fewer and fewer students

were reading at home. That's when they decided to provide protected independent reading time during the school day. Initially, the students who already loved reading were the ones who were most onboard. However, providing students support in choosing books engaged more of the reading community.

- Kim Hooper (@MommytoAg) is a high school librarian in Tennessee. She shared how her high school students do not have a designated time to visit the library. To counter this, she's offered to deliver students books of their choice; however, most students are not able to take her up on the offer. They've shared that they have so many assignments to complete at night, they don't have time to read for pleasure. (I thought this was a powerful reminder that teachers in every subject influence students' reading lives in some way.)

- Eric Carpenter (@_ericcarpenter1) is a school librarian in Georgia. He encourages making independent reading time the most sacred part of the school day by building your schedule around that time. Letting students know they will have silent reading time everyday even if there are assemblies or other events scheduled speaks volumes.

The insights above represent a small smattering of the ideas that were shared. Many educators indicated they were providing protected reading time right away each morning or following recess/lunch. The consensus was to steer clear of trying to schedule independent reading time at the end of the day because it's too unpredictable. Another theme several educators emphasized was being sure intervention and pull-out times do not supplant first-time core instruction.

I know that was a lot of information on *how* you might go about providing independent reading time to every reader. But it's also important to understand *why* it matters. The amount of time students spend reading is the single-greatest predictor of reading achievement

(Anderson, Wilson & Fielding, 1988; Krashen, 2004; NCTE, 2019). But time, alone, is not enough.

Providing choice and support during independent reading time maximizes the time students spend reading. Not all students have the skills needed to successfully self-select books (Allington, et al., 2010, Miller & Moss, 2013; ILA, 2018), or the skills to abandon books when appropriate. Besides that, at least once during the school day, all students deserve the opportunity to hold something that is 100% their choice (Allington & Gabriel, 2012), without somebody telling them it's too difficult, too easy, or not the right fit.

5. Ensure All Readers Feel Seen and Supported

When readers do not see themselves reflected in the books they read, or when the images are distorted, negative, or laughable, they learn a powerful lesson about their value in a reading community (Bishop, 1990). When you read stories that are representative of readers, you help readers feel seen and supported.

Dana Boyd is the 2016 Texas principal of the year and 2007 Texas teacher of the year. Many schools provide their staff professional development titles for book studies, but Dana takes a novel approach. She helps create connection and empathy through staff book studies that feature Young Adult books.

This past year, her staff read *Ghost Boys* by Jewell Parker Rhodes, *We Are Not From Here* by Jenny Tores Sanchez, and *Dry* by Jarrod Shusterman and Neal Shusterman. The feedback Dana received ranged from comments about never reading so many books in a school year before to comments about the books changing mindsets. Ensuring all students feel seen and supported requires a different mindset. The strongest reading communities are those that refuse to leave any student or group unseen. These reading communities are committed to having conversations about the books needed to create connection with readers.

6. Ask Questions that Illuminate the Reading Lives of Applicants During Interviews

If you want to create a community of readers, it makes sense to hire people who value reading, even if they're not officially reading teachers. It's more powerful for a student to see their Math, Science, or Music teacher as a reader than you might think. And the connection that's created when a student who loves physical education class receives a book recommendation from their PE teacher is pure magic.

Unfortunately, there's not a lot of information available on how to inject literacy-related questions into interviews that don't directly relate to being a reading or ELA teacher. I see this as an opportunity for literacy leaders to push the field forward. Even if you're not directly responsible for hiring, you can still make an impact. Some of the most effective changes we've made to our interview process came from the feedback of teacher-leaders serving on our interview teams.

Here is a list of six interview questions to help applicants illuminate their reading lives (see figure 5.6). The intent is to provide candidates the chance to talk about their relationship with reading and not to create a gotcha-type moment during an interview. I envision teams might choose one or two of the literacy-related questions and swap them out with a couple of traditional interview questions that are no longer helpful.

Most of the questions are pretty straightforward. However, the fifth question is written in two-parts. I'd suggest asking the first part and listening to an applicant's response before providing the follow-up question. The final question is what I refer to as a teaching question. It informs candidates and reminds the interview team about your school's commitment to reading. The information you glean from the question can also be put to good use when updating classroom libraries and your media collection.

6 INTERVIEW QUESTIONS
TO HELP APPLICANTS ILLUMINATE THEIR READING LIVES

▸ CAN YOU TELL US ABOUT A TIME WHEN YOUR READING LIFE ENHANCED YOUR TEACHING?

▸ CAN YOU TELL US ABOUT A BOOK YOU'VE USED TO HELP BUILD RELATIONSHIPS OR CREATE CLASSROOM COMMUNITY?

▸ CAN YOU THINK OF A BOOK YOU'VE READ RECENTLY THAT YOU'D RECOMMEND TO STUDENTS?

▸ IF YOU COULD CHOOSE A CHARACTER FROM ANY CHILDREN'S BOOK OR NOVEL TO HAVE AS A STUDENT WHO WOULD IT BE?

▸ CAN YOU SHARE A SPECIFIC LESSON YOU'VE TAUGHT THAT WENT WELL? IF YOU WERE TO INCORPORATE A PICTURE BOOK INTO THE LESSON WHAT BOOK WOULD YOU CHOOSE AND WHY?

▸ WE BELIEVE READING TRANSCENDS ALL SUBJECTS. CAN YOU SHARE SOME BOOKS OR THEMES WE COULD ADD TO OUR CLASSROOM AND SCHOOL LIBRARIES TO SUPPORT YOUR TEACHING?

FROM "THE 6 LITERACY LEVERS" BY BRAD GUSTAFSON (2021)

Figure 5.6: **Interview Questions**

7. Inject Literacy into Existing Events (and routines)

You don't need to add extra events to the calendar to champion literacy. A big part of building a reading community involves the traditions, events, and routines your school community already appreciates.

Students in our school love the annual carnival our Parent Teacher Association (PTA) organizes. Recently, our PTA added a "Book Swap" room where students can use carnival tickets to buy books. Now, in addition to looking forward to the Wacky Hair room, Soda Pop Toss, and traditional Fish Pond, students also look forward to a reading-themed room.

Julie Bloss is a principal in Oklahoma who tapped into the natural excitement many students have on their birthdays. She invites students to the library on their birthday or half birthday to self-select a book. The book choices are stored in a large box that's decorated like a birthday gift. Students love lifting the lid and seeing the "presents" inside the giant gift box.

To stockpile enough high-quality books for students to choose from, Julie relies on her school's Buy One Get One (BOGO) book fair and other deals advertised online. This tradition is more than putting books in the hands of students. It's about creating connection.

Sometimes this connection involves adding a special note inside the books students choose. Other times, it's taking a photo with a student or featuring their book choice on Julie's school YouTube show. The relational ripples and connection that's created from tapping into a student's special day makes this a tradition that Julie looks forward to just as much as her students.

Another tradition many elementary-aged students look forward to is Valentine's Day. One year, my son and I built a working Turbo Toilet 2000 for his Valentine's Day box at school. The toilet handle even triggered the mail slot to open (see figure 5.7). The project created quite the buzz during my son's class Valentine's party, but it also showcased his love for Dav Pilkey's books.

This got me thinking: what if schools gave kids time during the school day to create valentine boxes celebrating their favorite books and authors? Dedicating class time to the project would ensure every student had the support and supplies needed to participate in the celebration.

8. Invite Authors into Your School and Treat Them Like Celebrities
Our school community has prioritized bringing in diverse authors who allow all students to see themselves reflected in the books they're reading. One of the things I've always struggled with is celebrating special guests without breaking the bank. I'm not talking about compensating authors for their time and hard work. I'm talking about celebrating authors in a manner that makes them feel special.

Figure 5.7: **Literacy-Inspired Valentine Box**

One of the things our team tried was turning the framed gallery in our main entryway into an author appreciation zone. This allows us to amplify the creativity of students while also showing visiting authors how excited we are to have them in our school. When Hena Kahn visited, our art teacher and media specialist collaborated on a display that contained several student art pieces inspired by her books (see figure 5.8 and figure 5.9).

We also started giving visiting authors an honorary library card (see figure 5.10). The cards are presented in the same spirit as giving a distinguished guest the keys to a city. The back of each card contains the following message:

Reading is at the heart of everything we do, and our media center is the heart of our school. You've made our heart better and we're forever indebted. Please consider yourself a lifetime card-carrying Greenwood Grizzly.

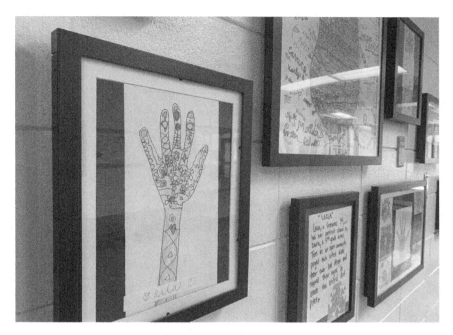

Figures 5.8 - 5.9: **Author Appreciation Zone**

Figures 5.10: **Honorary Library Card**

Modeling how to treat authors as distinguished guests sends a strong message. Inviting students to be part of the process catapults culture forward.

9. Plan Opportunities for Families to Connect Around Reading Throughout the Year

    A strong bridge between school and home is essential to building a community of readers (Baker & Moss, 1993). Dr. Alice Lee is the principal at Richmond Street School in California. She found that maintaining this bridge can be incredibly challenging at times—like in the middle of a global pandemic when the access families had to schools was restricted.

    Instead of canceling their Family Literacy Night, her team created an opportunity for their community to come together via a virtual

"Masked Reader" event (see figure 5.11). Several staff members dressed up in disguises and read to students online. Families were invited to interact in the chat and type in their guesses about who the masked readers were. The event was a huge success. It offered some much-needed connection for families during a time when many people were feeling extremely isolated.

As innovative as Alice and her team's idea was, I'm more impressed with how they are working to build a strong bridge with families throughout the year. Literacy Night is a big deal, but it's just one of many connections they make over the course of the school year. They bring readers together using a principal's book club as well as a whole-school book club. Staff share their reading identities and get to know students' identities as readers.

10. Build a Budget that Prioritizes the School Media Program and Classroom Libraries

I don't know about you, but when I think about school budgets my mind tends to go to spreadsheets and funding formulas. It is important

Figure 5.11: **Masked Reader Flyer**

to keep a connection to who the budget supports and the types of experiences you want readers to have.

I remember tucking in one of my kids when she was in elementary school. We were having a bedtime conversation about a book she requested at school. She was interested in genetics and had asked one of her teachers if they could help her find a book about DNA. The answer she received was a solid "No." At least that's what my daughter walked away hearing.

When she was telling me about this during a bedtime conversation, I remember thinking, *I want to lead a school that always tries to connect kids to books they want to read.* At the time, I wasn't sure how I might be able to help with this, so I started paying attention to the things I had the most influence over. Like how our school budget is created.

We started by adding a modest line-item in the budget to support innovation. The following year, we made this line-item even more accessible by streamlining things. All a teacher needed to do to access the innovation budget was send a one-sentence email to me. Each year, we iterated the budget and process in support of the visionary work teachers were leading. Fast forward to today, and we're currently budgeting between $500-$700 per grade-level to provide a boost to classroom libraries.

Updating the budget to make reading more of a priority has eliminated some of the structural barriers to book access, updated classroom collections, and helped teachers be able to say "Yes" more often when students request books. Instead of calling this an innovation budget, I'm thinking we should call it our *connection* budget!

11. Design an Environment that Celebrates Reading

Creating connection through design can be done virtually anywhere in a school. Indoors and outdoors. The following examples show a variety of ways literacy leaders are leveraging design to strengthen their reading communities.

One of our physical education teachers, Mary Hurwitz, has maintained a giant word wall in our gym for years (see figure 5.12). The words are printed on large street signs that reinforce key health and movement concepts. I love seeing how students who don't particularly care for reading yet, connect with the giant word wall in the gym. It's as though being in an environment they associate with their strengths and passions propels their reading motivation.

Josh Stumpenhorst is a middle school teacher-librarian in Illinois. Although he's creating community in the library, it doesn't always involve books. In fact, one of his favorite design features in the library might surprise you.

Every spring, Josh's school transforms the library into a giant game room and arcade to coincide with the March Madness Basketball Tournament. The game room and arcade are open to all students

Figure 5.12: **Giant Gym Word Wall**

during their lunch periods and study halls. Josh sets up board games on tables and a couple of Nintendo Switches. Students can choose to play games like Mario Kart, Rocket League, or Smash Brothers. They also have five Raspberry Pi running retro games on large flat screens, and even purchased some electronic components so students can build their own controllers.

I love how Josh is able to celebrate some of the other passions and interests readers have through this idea. Besides that, designing the library to be a gathering place for everyone creates community.

Dr. Mary Howard is an educator, author, and speaker. A few years ago, I was reading her blog, *Literacy Lenses: Focusing on Literacy Work that Matters*, and noticed an inspiring image (see figure 5.13). The picture showed principal Mike Oliver's office decked floor to ceiling with books. And not just any books—picture books, chapter books, and

Figure 5.13: **Literacy Leader's Office**

professional development books. A closer look at the picture reveals a beautiful array of diverse titles with powerful messages.

From the moment I saw the picture, I knew I wanted my office to be something that reflected my passion for reading while also celebrating the different strengths, cultures, and stories in our school. Being more intentional with how the design of my office celebrates literacy has created unexpected connections with visitors. Hat tip to Mike Oliver for being a literacy leader and positive role model to me and many others.

Empowering students to be part of the design process is important. This can be done in countless ways, but I've noticed many students seem to love literacy-themed door decorating. I always appreciate how anyone with a door can participate. I also love how literacy-themed door decorating inspires creativity in readers.

It's always fun to see the different books and approaches classrooms choose (see figure 5.14). Students in one class converted the window slat into a miniature diorama that offered a magical glimpse into the book they chose. The shared experience of decorating classroom doors created connection and led to a book-related buzz that could be heard in the hallways for weeks.

Jennifer Brown is a principal at Hurley Elementary School in North Carolina. Her staff is striving to create the conditions in which students *want* to read. A big part of their strategy involves being intentional with how readers experience the physical environment. But it also involves connecting with other literacy leaders to share successful ideas and strategies. Jennifer is part of a robust online reading community and adapted the following idea from colleagues there.

She worked with her school and the broader community to create an outdoor reading oasis for students (see figure 5.15). They installed a grid-pattern of 6x6 posts and hung 24 reading hammocks from them. After that, they added some overhead shade and introduced the new space to readers in their school. The outdoor transformation at Jennifer's school would not have been possible without teamwork or community

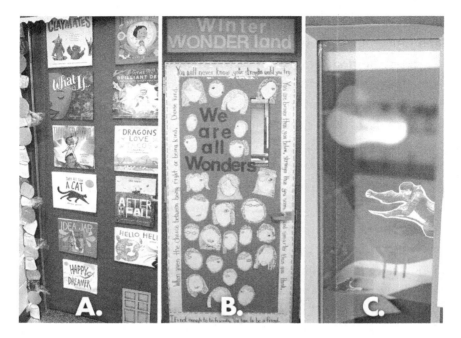

Figure 5.14: **Door Decorating**

support. There is nothing quite like seeing the joy on students' faces as they enter a space genuinely excited to read while hanging out together.

12.   Actively Share Your Reading Life with Others

Actively sharing your reading life is about showing up as your authentic self. In the spaces you already occupy. It's not about inventing new work for yourself or others. You don't need to become a walking billboard for books either. It's more about looking for meaningful opportunities to share your reading identity in the things you're already doing.

Earlier in the book I shared how my friend, Dr. LaQuita Outlaw, often travels the hallways in her

> Showing up as your authentic self is your gift to others— even when you're empty handed.

Figures 5.15: **Outdoor Reading Oasis**

school carrying a book. Sometimes carrying a book creates opportunities for her to share what she's reading. Other times she simply arrives
at her destination with a book. If you try this idea, there will be days
you forget your book or don't have time to grab it. And that's okay, too.
Showing up as your authentic self is your gift to others—even when
you're empty handed.

Like LaQuita, I try to share my reading life in different ways. I
ditched my traditional business cards and created principal baseball-style
cards several years ago (see figure 5.16). The theme of these principal

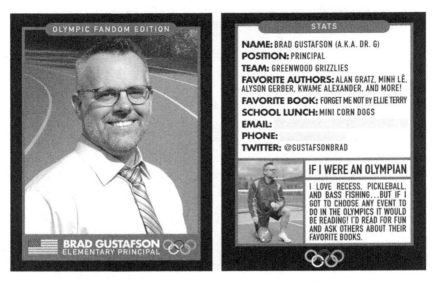

Figure 5.16: **Business Cards that Create Connection (Front and Back)**

cards changes each year, but I always find a way to weave my reading life and favorite books into the stats section on the back of the cards.

Feedback from families and the response we've received from students over the years has been really positive. In many ways, the cards have served as a relational springboard. Whether it's reminiscing about favorite Olympic sports, swapping school lunch stories, or talking about personal connections we have to different authors, sharing my reading life has helped me create connection.

13. Create Additional Connection Using Tools that are Relevant to Readers

I'm always a little hesitant to share specific examples when talking about tools. This idea is not about prescribing a particular tool; it's about being intentional in selecting tools relevant to readers and in using those tools purposefully. To create *connection*.

Many schools use book brackets to create connection and build community (see figure 5.17). Oftentimes, these book tournaments coincide with college basketball tournaments that take place in March. Whether these book brackets are printed on a paper template like the one I provided, or sprawled across a cafeteria wall, the conversation and energy they create around which books should move forward each week is electric.

I've seen many reading teachers print picture book covers or images of the books they've read aloud in class to fill in the brackets. Entire schools have done this, too. I'm intrigued about how a literacy leader who teaches math, music, or science might create a book bracket using trade books connected to their content area. Using a tool like this can create endless opportunities for students to connect in different ways.

Figure 5.17: **Book-Bracket Tournament Template**

I was talking with my good friend and literacy leader, Liz Garden, about the tournament of books concept and she shared an incredible story. Her school had been doing a month-long tournament and readers were dialed in. Each morning, they would check the tournament bracket posted in the main display case for updates. On the final day of the tournament, Liz and her assistant principal at the time, who also happened to be an incredible literacy leader, Patty Hurley, announced the winning book in a big way and students loved it.

The two literacy leaders got inside the display case and struck a pose while holding the winning book. When students arrived in the morning to check the bracket, they were surprised to see their principals frozen in place holding the winning book. The connection and energy were unlike anything they had experienced before. Liz recalls the experience as one of her favorite principal moments ever—mostly because of how her reading community responded.

Figure 5.18: **Tournament of Books Display Case**

As I was chatting with Liz about the experience, she shared something else that caught my attention. The display case that brought everyone together over the course of their school's book-bracket activity was important for another reason. Over the years, Liz and her team have used the display case to connect with readers in a variety of ways. You could say the case itself is known to be a tool and space that's relevant to readers.

Social media is another tool and space that is motivating and relevant to many students. At the same time, many educators have yet to embrace social media. Even if social media has been a non-starter for you in the past, I encourage you to consider it with fresh eyes. First and foremost, integrating social media into your literacy leadership toolbox will ultimately help you help readers.

By using specific hashtags, you can quickly find fellow readers and the specific literacy content you're looking for. Whether that be book recommendations, conversation threads, or collecting ideas. But hashtags aren't just for consuming content from other literacy leaders. When you add a hashtag to your social media posts, other members of the broader reading community can find what you're sharing more easily.

Here are a few ways to tap into social media as a tool to connect with literacy leaders around the world:

- *Interact with an existing hashtag*

There are several existing hashtags on social media that are home to a robust community of readers. In these spaces you can see book recommendations from other literacy leaders, join discussions, and share your own reading life. I'd suggest searching for #NerdyBookClub, #PernilleRecommends, #ReadThisNow, #BookLove #TeachWrite #ClassroomBookADay #BookADay #InclusiveBooks #LiteracyLever and #GraphicNovelsAreRealBooks to name a few.

- *Create your own hashtag*

Starting a new hashtag is a great way to learn and grow with other readers in your school community. We used our school's initials and added the word "reads" to create a literacy-themed hashtag (#GWreads). In addition to helping me stay more connected to other literacy leaders in our school, I love how the hashtag is filled with so many pictures showing smiling readers.

- *Join our reading community at #LiteracyLever*

By virtue of the fact you're reading this book, you automatically have something in common with other literacy leaders. Why not introduce yourself by posting a selfie with the book, asking a question, or sharing an idea? Just be sure to add the hashtag to your post so we can find and follow you on social media (#LiteracyLever).

14. Booktalk, Booktalk, Booktalk!

In a reading community, people talk about what they're reading. It's not the only thing they talk about, but it's definitely an important part of the culture. In chapter four, I shared that booktalks are one of the most versatile tools available when it comes to literacy leadership. I also focused more on some of the technical components of booktalks, like how to create and share them. One thing I may not have emphasized enough is the connective power that rests in talking about books. Booktalks build community.

Literacy leaders create community and activate a passion for reading by sharing the books they love. These conversations need not feel complicated. When booktalks are simple, organic, and authentic, there is a very good chance readers will experience a feeling of connection. However, when booktalks feel forced or are used to shut down conversations, they have the opposite effect.

Earlier in this book, I introduced you to the team of teachers working at Springside Elementary in the Alpine (UT) School District. You might recall how their journey involved a series of organic invitations which eventually led them to being a positive, literacy-leading force in their school and beyond. In one of my conversations with the team, I asked them how they kept booktalks authentic and something students actually want to be part of.

The Springside team started by sharing how students tend to appreciate hearing about the things their classmates are excited about. Their teachers, principals, and parents can talk about a book until they're blue in the face, but a heartfelt endorsement from a friend carries a special kind of connection. This realization has helped guide the team's commitment to student voice and curiosity. If the adults in your school are the only ones talking about books, your reading community might not be as inclusive as you think. Don't allow booktalks to become glorified lectures.

> If the adults in your school are the only ones talking about books, your reading community might not be as inclusive as you think.

The power of the catapult can be found in how it engages all readers in a way that's meaningful to each reader. The 4th-grade team from Springside shared how they encourage students to choose when and how they share (or don't share) a book. Their approach evidences the belief that booktalks aren't an assignment; they're a privilege.

The Springside team tries to provide readers a variety of book-sharing options. Some students add to book-graffiti walls and others display drawings of books or characters they love. Even culminating projects come with an array of choices that range from stop-motion videos and book-cover art to designing posters. Readers have even brought in everyday objects from home that represented the books and characters they wanted to talk about.

The result of the team's differentiated approach to booktalks has been a more inclusive culture. The team is leading a community of readers who want to engage in conversations about books.

Students are empowered to enter into conversations and express their reading experiences in creative ways...which further strengthens the community.

15. Celebrate Students' Interests and Culture

A reading community that denies the interests of readers is destined to become a ghost town. Reading communities that see and celebrate readers' strengths and backgrounds will boom. The things that build relationships, empathy, and understanding should not be feared. They must be revered.

Celebrating the strengths and culture of one person or group doesn't mean you're taking anything away from anyone else. It means you're creating space for more than one story. It also means you're open to the possibility that growth is needed for some students to feel safe, seen, and accepted.

To truly push the field forward, literacy leaders need to engage in honest and ongoing conversations about how and where this work is being done well and where it needs to be done better.

An area in which I faltered for many years involved the authors I celebrated on my own bookshelves. There were genres I enjoyed and authors that felt familiar, but I wasn't very intentional about reading books that different students could see themselves in. My own personal reading choices may not seem like too big a deal until you think about them in terms of missed opportunities. Conversations that never occurred. Connection that was never felt.

Fortunately, the rest of our team has always worked hard to celebrate the interests and culture of students. Not only as represented in the books in our collection, but also in the authors who visit our school. Seeing their intentionality in this area has helped me understand why it matters so much.

I'll never forget one of the times Lehman Riley, author of the *Papa Lemon* historical fiction series, finished presenting to students in our media center. I was chatting with a few readers as they were making their way back to class when I overheard one student say, "He looks like me." He was talking to a friend, but his words were filled with awe and appreciation.

I still get a little choked up just thinking about how the student responded. Lehman is a Black man, and the experience reminded me how important it is to be intentional in creating an inclusive reading community that celebrates each and every reader. During read alouds. Book purchases. Author visits. And so much more.

Literacy leaders look for ways to celebrate the interests, backgrounds, and cultures of all readers. When you fail to do this, the damage is real. Stories are excluded. Engagement decreases. Opportunities are missed. Worse yet, some readers can be made to feel like they are less or not part of the community.

If you have students who have not engaged with reading or your reading community yet, don't discount the importance of learning more about their interests and culture or in helping them see themselves in books, authors, and reading experiences. Don't blame students who feel like reading is unfashionable or not for them—especially when the books and assignments they must choose from don't reflect their interests and strengths.

Rhonda Jenkins is a Media Center Director who strives to create an authentic connection between readers, books, and each other. She understands the language of student voice and seeks to create enriched literacy experiences that empower students to share their culture and interests with each other. One of the ways she does this is through the intersection of literacy and fashion.

Rhonda helps readers design digital versions of literacy-inspired clothing they might like to wear (see figure 5.19). Fashion is one way many students like to express themselves. The *Lit Threads* they design motivate them to interact with books and each other in a way that makes them feel seen.

JUDE, A 12 YEAR OLD,
WILL GUIDE YOU THROUGH HER
  HEARTBREAKING JOURNEY.
SHE HAS TO FLEE
AND LEAVE BEHIND
  HER FATHER,
  HER BROTHER,
  HER HOME,
  EVERYTHING SHE KNOWS AND LOVES
  TO BE SAFE FROM
  THE VIOLENCE IN HER
  WAR TORN COUNTRY, SYRIA.
  IN THE USA,
  SHE STILL HAS TO DEAL WITH
  SCARY PREJUDICES
  THAT CHILDREN SHOULD
  NEVER HAVE TO FACE!
  YOU'LL FEAR FOR HER,
  CHEER FOR HER,
  AND BE PROUD OF HOW SHE
  CHERISHES HER CULTURE!

JASMINE WARGA

I'D WEAR THIS
GREAT BOOK
ANY DAY!

Figure 5.19: **Lit Threads**

In case you're interested in trying something similar, Rhonda uses Photoshop to make the T-shirt portion of the picture transparent and then saves it as a png, jpeg, or gif. She created a folder with transparent T-shirts you can use at https://bit.ly/30CoZQK. The rest of the design process can be completed in a few steps using your favorite design software:

+ Find an image of a book and insert that image into a new document.

+ Upload the transparent T-shirt image you selected from Rhonda's folder.

+ Adjust and resize the book image under the transparent T-shirt so it fits relatively well.

+ Insert additional shapes, colors, or patterns around the book image until the transparent T-shirt is completely filled in.

Selecting colors and creating shapes that complement the cover image is part of the fun.
+ Add text boxes around your fashion design to share how you feel about the book or why you'd wear it.
+ Be sure to cite any images you use.
+ Finalize your design in Google Drawing.
+ Download and save the design as a jpg or png so you can share it with others.

As I reflect on this idea, I'm also envisioning students who might be interested in creating book-inspired race car designs. My guess is that the process Rhonda shared above could be used to support a wide variety of readers' interests.

A Word of Caution

There's a difference between creating enriched literacy experiences and trying to improve a mediocre assignment or practice. Making mediocre assignments better doesn't create an inclusive reading community. Seeing strengths and tapping into students' interests goes beyond the assignments we attach to their reading lives.

One of the most inclusive and reader-centric things you can do is scale back on the superfluous things you attach to students' reading lives. The very thing a child might be most interested in could be "just reading." Be intentional with what you ask readers to do. Ask yourself if there's anything you might be able to remove from their reading lives. Seek their feedback. Listen.

Leaders who plan professional development would do well to heed the same cautionary advice. Just because you *can* ask a learner to do something with what they've just read or learned doesn't mean you always *should*. Too often, professional development involves adding to people's to-do lists with not enough time for reflection, choice, and authentic implementation. I'm as guilty of this as the next school leader.

Is it any wonder many educators associate professional development with something that's done *to them* instead of something they would choose for themselves? Don't let this be the prevailing feeling readers walk away from school with.

Putting the Catapult into Action

There are plenty of other meaningful things you and your team can do to champion relationships, connection, and community. The most important thing to keep in mind is that the catapult is most effective when it's leveraged together.

The Literacy Walk & Talk approach (see figure 5.20) is a collaborative, strengths-based tool to help you and your team co-create a reading community. It follows the popular 3-2-1 format for feedback which places the most emphasis on looking for practices to celebrate and spread. Eventually, Walk & Talk conversations funnel to finding something you're curious about.

This provides a place holder for colleagues to ask about practices and ideas they want to learn more about. It also creates a space where honest and complex questions can be broached in a non-evaluative manner.

In looking at the Walk & Talk approach, you will find a prompt written in each of the rows (i.e., What did you see, hear, or feel...). This prompt is intended to help ground conversations in objective observations (i.e., what you *see* and *hear*) while leaving the door open to discuss your emotional connection to what you observe (i.e., how you *feel*).

The Walk & Talk approach is best completed by three to four people who agree in advance to focus on similar look-fors. I recommend using the list of *15 Ways to Co-Create a Reading Community* to help guide your decisions about the look-fors you'll be walking and talking about. You could also consider circling one or two specific things from

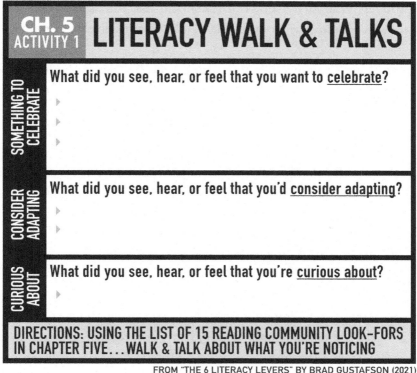

Figure 5.20: **Literacy Walk & Talks (Activity)**

the list of fifteen and inviting your colleagues to look for those things when they visit your space and/or observe you interacting with readers.

The Walk & Talk approach is intended to take place over a period of months. I suggest scheduling a few different times to connect with the same colleagues for your walk and talks. It works well to schedule your first walk & talk during a time when instruction is not occurring. Finding a non-instructional time for your first Walk & Talk will make it easier for you to absorb the environment. Future Walk & Talks could certainly take place during instructional time if your team makes the necessary arrangements, but they could also involve looking at some of the less-examined aspects of leadership like your school's budget, media collection, or any other look for you want to dive deeper into.

1. Connect with a colleague or group of colleagues to plan a few different times to try the Literacy Walk & Talks approach together.

2. Depending on the size of your team or department, you may need to split into several smaller groups of 3-4 people.

3. Walk & Talks can be done anywhere and anytime, so work together to identify the times, spaces, and things each of you would like feedback on. Again, the list of 15 Ways to Co-Create a Reading Community can serve as a menu you can choose from when identifying your look-fors.

4. As you walk and talk about what you're noticing, jot down notes using the activity template. If you're in a group of three people, but one of you is actively leading an activity with readers, the remaining two people in your group would obviously do the noticing and writing. If a Walk & Talk is being done during a lesson or staff meeting, the bulk of the walking and talking would most likely come after the lesson or meeting.

5. Plan a time to debrief together after each round of the Literacy Walk & Talks approach is completed. During this time, discuss what was directly observed, ask questions, and seek ideas on how to enhance your leadership. Talk about how the experience felt and how readers responded. This is also the perfect time to commit to the practices you and your team want to provide all readers (e.g., regular independent reading time and choice).

Questions to Push the Field Forward

- What processes, procedures, or systems need to be updated to ensure each and every reader feels seen and supported within your reading community?

+ How can the practice of getting to know readers as people be converted into an inclusive action plan?

Leverage Your Literacy Leadership Schoolwide

When I talk about the power of connection and relationships, I'm not dismissing the importance of reading skills and achievement. Literacy leaders need to ensure this work is about establishing a robust reading community *and* helping every reader develop the fundamental reading skills needed to be successful. Both these things are unlikely to happen without a plan.

If you've served in education long enough, you know what happens when you don't make relationships and community an explicit priority. Conversations about standardized tests and assessment creep tends to take over. This reminds me of the story I shared earlier in this chapter about attending a national principal conference to hear Kwame Alexander speak.

If the *only* thing that mattered to me was scores, I never would have catapulted across a packed arena of principals in an attempt to get closer to Kwame Alexander. I was compelled to take that leap due to the power of relationships, connection, and members of my reading community.

If your team's goals or school improvement plan do not tap into this type of energy and connection, the readers you serve will be less inclined to take the leap and connect with reading and each other on a deeper level.

Challenge yourself to create a plan to strengthen and invest in your school's reading community. Collaborate with your leadership team and/or colleagues to create a plan that addresses the foundational reading skills and instruction all students need, as well as relationships and connection.

Start small and identify an aspect or idea from the list of 15 Ways to Co-Create a Reading Community. Whatever you choose, make it something you can start focusing on (or implementing) tomorrow. There is power in collectively agreeing to a first step, but sometimes action requires everyone to choose a play from the playbook that's meaningful to them. This is one reason why I identified fifteen ways to co-create a reading community. There are several different entry points for staff who are leading in different roles.

After your school takes its first step, collaborate with your leadership team or other colleagues to move forward on the rest of your plan. This could involve introducing additional ideas or it might mean that you focus on a single strategy together for an entire year to take that strategy and work deeper. For example, if your school wanted to start by making booktalks a priority, it would make a lot of sense to take this commitment deeper every single month instead of introducing competing ideas.

Be sure part of your schoolwide process involves conversations about what you want your reading community to look, sound, and feel like at the end of the school year. Much like the compass, this vision will help inform the smaller steps and decisions about professional learning experiences. When the small steps that individuals are taking align with a bigger, shared vision, culture catapults forward.

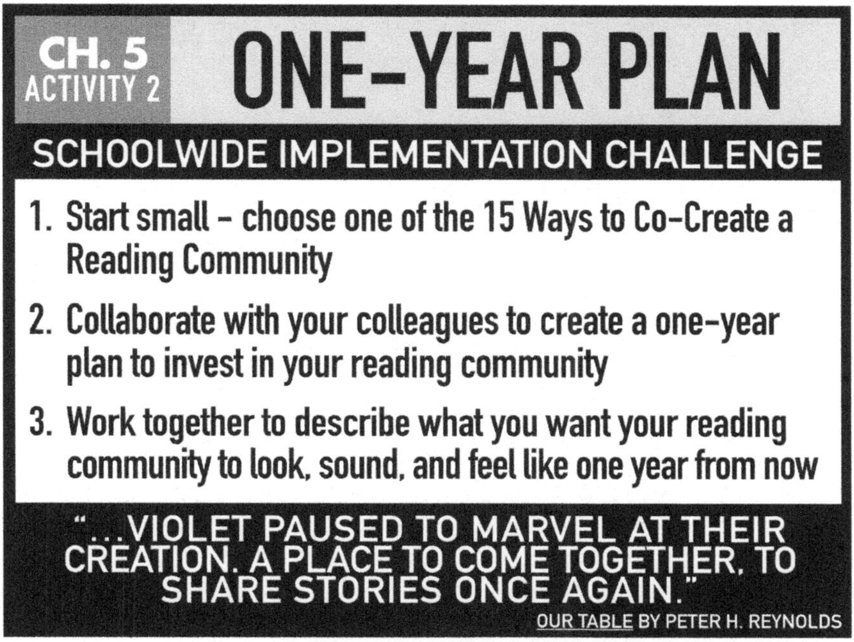

CH. 5
ACTIVITY 2 ONE-YEAR PLAN

SCHOOLWIDE IMPLEMENTATION CHALLENGE

1. Start small – choose one of the 15 Ways to Co-Create a Reading Community

2. Collaborate with your colleagues to create a one-year plan to invest in your reading community

3. Work together to describe what you want your reading community to look, sound, and feel like one year from now

"...VIOLET PAUSED TO MARVEL AT THEIR CREATION. A PLACE TO COME TOGETHER, TO SHARE STORIES ONCE AGAIN."

OUR TABLE BY PETER H. REYNOLDS

FROM "THE 6 LITERACY LEVERS" BY BRAD GUSTAFSON (2021)

Figure 5.21: **Schoolwide Implementation Challenge**

CHAPTER 6

The Collage

Imagine this: You're on your way back to the café for your first book club meeting with Dayo and Lydia. It's been a week since you last saw them. When you arrive, Lydia is standing outside engrossed in a phone conversation. She's wearing a T-shirt with a stack of books screen-printed on the front. Next to the books in retro lettering are the words, "Book 'em Dayo." The meeting hasn't even started yet, but you secretly decide she's the coolest person in the book club.

As you walk inside, Dayo waves you over to your table. There are several books spread across the tabletop. You scan the covers and ask, "What's today's item?" Dayo pauses to consider the question then abruptly leaves the table. He retrieves a polaroid camera from behind the café counter and returns to the table. You venture a guess but realize it sounds more like a question as the words escape your lips. "A picture?"

Dayo shakes his head and smiles as if to suggest you should keep guessing. Then, he stretches his arm out, smiles...and waits. It takes a few seconds to register; he's waiting to take a picture. You lean in and smile.

A blank picture appears from underneath the camera. Dayo removes it from the camera and instinctively starts to shake it. Then, he clears his throat and says, "Of course there are other items." He points emphatically to the picture and says, "But you. *You* are the lever." The way he emphasizes the word "you" feels like a call to action.

Then, he reaches behind the table and adds your picture to the collection of polaroid photos on the wall. You smile when you notice the picture next to yours. It's of the young boy with the marshmallow mustache. He's hugging that caterpillar book. There's an arm wrapped around his shoulders, and you know who it belongs to. You start to imagine the boy's mom and all the time they spent reading together in and out of the café.

You allow your eyes to scan the rest of the collage. You find Lydia and eventually Dayo. You begin to peel back some of the layers of the collage to reveal additional faces. And stories. You lean in closer when you notice somebody holding a walking stick. It's your mystery-reading mentor. You smile and look back towards Dayo.

Knowing you're part of the collage now stirs something in you. Dayo smiles and asks, "So what should *we* do now?" The way he emphasizes the word "we" makes it feel like the most powerful word in the world.

- What would you do next if you decided to fully embrace the fact that *you* are an important lever in the lives of readers?
- What's the difference between a collage and a selfie? Why might this distinction be important?
- What's another lever you might use as a literacy leader (i.e., stories, listening, research)? How does the lever work?

Figure 6.1: **The Collage Defined**

"My courage gives you permission to be courageous."
~Anthony Muhammed

From Story to Practice

You are the lever. Your posture towards literacy has the power to con-nect, grow, and include. To persuade and compel. But you are not in this work alone. The collage you're connected to is capable of serving readers in a way no individual ever could.

In the introduction of this book, I told you there is not a single reader in your school who doesn't deserve to be seen, supported, and included. And I meant it. What I may not have mentioned is the importance of engaging your entire team and school in the mission and work. You are the lever, but the collage is critical.

Literacy leadership is a symbiotic relationship. The levers work together and respond differently depending on how you and your team apply them. The compass you carry matters. But it's nothing apart from your leadership and the discernment of your team. The invitations you accept and extend matter because the work you're committed to matters. The walking stick, utility knife, and catapult will enhance your effectiveness, but *you* are the lever. And the people who are part of your school's literacy collage can be, too.

This chapter focuses on actionable steps you and your team can take. Starting today. In the few remaining pages we have together, I intend to help you with these next steps and more. I'll share a tool you and your colleagues can use to reflect on where your literacy leadership is right now, and help you initiate conversations about where you want to go. I'll also provide you several options, or pathways, from which to choose. But before I do, I want to share a story of hope.

There's a very good chance you're reading this book in close proximity to somebody who doesn't see themselves as a reader, let alone a literacy lever—yet. (That person might even be you.) No matter what your colleagues feel about literacy right now, never write them off. The collage isn't complete until everyone is included. So never say never.

Never Say Never

When I was a senior in high school, I had a crush on the captain of the girls' high school soccer team. She had a deep faith, strong spirit, and was beautiful on the inside and out. She still is.

We went on to create a life together that's been better than anything I could have ever imagined. *Except for this one thing.* Although we didn't explicitly address this *one thing* in our wedding vows, we always operated with an understanding that we weren't "dog people." Neither of us were. And not just in a past-tense kind of way.

I'm scared of dogs.
They bite.
They bark.
They're expensive.
They lick you,
After licking themselves and other stuff.
They make it difficult to travel.
They smell,
But they smell even worse when they're wet.
And they make walking barefoot in the backyard risky business.

Not to mention, when I was in middle school, I had to walk by a neighbor's dog every morning to get to my bus stop. Most days that dog just sat there and terrified me. But occasionally, it would come after me. It got to the point that I needed to ask my mom to walk me to the bus stop. As a middle schooler.

So, you can see why I thought our family would never get a dog. Ever.

But sometimes things get complicated—and better at the same time. My high school sweetheart and I went on to have three incredible kids together. The fact we had kids didn't lessen my resolve to live a dog-free lifestyle. Because facts are facts, and we still weren't dog people.

It wasn't until our oldest daughter was diagnosed with high-functioning Autism that I started to understand how a four-legged companion could be helpful to her. When I say, "I started to understand," what I really mean is that my wife helped me understand. She invited me into the idea that a dog would be very good for our daughter's development.

And when something is good for your kids all bets are off. (You might as well start calling me the *dog whisperer* now because you can probably guess where this is going.) My wife and I did some research and learned that there are a few different dog breeds that are especially good matches for children with Autism. And because our longing to help our daughter develop deeper connections with the world was more important than our silly no-dog stance, we welcomed a Golden-doodle named "Willow" into our home. And now, we are dog people.

Willow has changed our family on multiple levels. On more than one occasion, our daughter has welcomed us into her innermost thoughts and said, "Willow is my best friend." Times like this are pure-parenting gold.

When I look back at what changed from the time my wife and I would *never* be dog people to now, my mind goes to one thing. Had it not been for my wife's wisdom, open mind, and selfless leadership, I don't think I would have experienced such a profound shift in my own thinking. She was the lever who invited me into a world I never thought I'd be part of. And not only did she invite me into this world, somehow, I'm the one recommending dogs to other people now, too. Even though I said I'd never be a dog person. So, never say never. Not to yourself or anyone else.

Confessions of a Literacy Leader

If I can become a dog person, I'm extremely confident your colleagues can grow as readers. And leaders. But this is because I wasn't always the reading leader our students deserve either. I always felt as though I was supportive of our school's literacy efforts, but I came to realize my support was more passive than anything else. My posture towards literacy leadership could have been described as neutral. Maybe even a little detached—at least compared to some of the other initiatives we were leading.

I may have been quick to give the greenlight to our school's reading champions, but my level of engagement was not meaningful or active enough to help move the needle when it came to our culture and literacy practices. You could say I relied more on delegating that responsibility to the people I viewed as more equipped or more responsible for reading.

As I've reflected on my journey and transformation over the years, I've come to realize my approach may have been well-intentioned. If I'm being *generous* (to myself), you could say that I had a strong desire to empower others and build capacity. But if I'm being *honest*, it would have been much more effective for me to be actively engaged and actively supporting, modeling, and leading our work related to literacy while still empowering others.

Thankfully, the literacy leaders we had on staff never gave up on me. They steadfastly modeled the things literacy leaders do and invited me into the world of reading on a regular basis. This helped me see the very next steps I needed to take to be the type of leader that the readers in our school needed me to be.

Your Literacy Leadership Posture

I was leading in an imbalanced manner. My posture may have been positive, but I wasn't actively engaged in the work of literacy leadership. The difference now is that I have a more nuanced understanding of literacy leadership. I didn't do anything fancy to come to this realization. I did reflect on the things I was delegating and the things I was doing. In previous years, I assumed the literacy leaders around me were more capable and more competent. Maybe even more responsible for doing the work.

It wasn't until I realized I had a responsibility to lead differently that my engagement with our school's literacy work increased. And so did my literacy learning. Which reminds me of something our district's associate superintendent often says, "It's okay to be where you are. It's not okay to stay there." This activity will help you better understand your posture towards literacy leadership and empower you to keep growing.

1. Start by looking at the continuum as it applies to your literacy leadership (see figure 6.2). Reflect upon where you see yourself showing up. Note: Neither end of the continuum is good or bad, so try to reflect honestly on how you approach literacy leadership most often.

2. Place an "X" in the box you feel shows where you are on the continuum.

3. Next, write down a couple of examples or reasons underneath the "X." These could include work you do on a daily basis, projects you're currently part of, or conversations you've had.

4. Last, try to imagine what it might look like for you to show up in different places on the continuum. Imagine your "X" moving and envision what might have to change for you to feel more comfortable showing up in different places/modes. Remember,

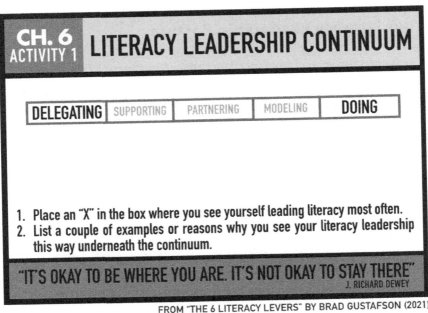

Figure 6.2: **Literacy Leadership Continuum (Activity)**

182

there isn't a single place on the continuum that is bad, as I'll explain in a second.

Continuums can be helpful because each incremental step shows nuanced differences between two things that are actually quite different. For example, there's a nuanced difference between delegating and supporting. But moving from *delegating* to *doing* is significantly different.

For what it's worth, you could substitute or add to the words I placed between *delegating* and *doing*. A case could certainly be made for adding incremental steps like "empowering" and "cheerleading" somewhere on the delegating side of things. The point is to reflect on how you're showing up and how that might be impacting readers. As I previously mentioned, delegating and doing are not dichotomous. Both matter.

Here's where this gets really interesting. You will want to factor in the needs and readiness level of the people you serve to guide decisions about what you're delegating and what you're doing. Sometimes you'll even find yourself on both ends of the continuum simultaneously. Being nimble in your leadership style improves the performance of others (Raza & Sikandar, 2018).

While you're practicing this situational leadership, you will want to be aware of the positive and negative aspects of whatever approach you decide is right for a situation. In other words, deciding to delegate or do is only half the battle.

If you're providing leadership in a situation where another person has the prerequisite skills and readiness level to assume some of the responsibilities, *delegation* could be an effective response because it involves empowerment, cheerleading, trust, collaboration, accountability (to self and others), and active support. However, if you're not intentional with how you delegate, it could also include unfairly releasing responsibility, overburdening others, disengagement, and dwindling results. These are some of the potential negative aspects of delegating that can present themselves depending on who you're delegating to and what your level of engagement is in the process.

The same holds true for *doing*. If you're providing leadership to a group who needs more modeling, direct instruction, and feedback, it probably makes sense to plan on doing an appropriate amount of the work. In this situation, doing would be effective because it involves modeling, partnership, and helping to achieve the desired results. However, if you're not intentional, doing the work could also result in excluding others, missing opportunities to build capacity, or stifling the creativity and contributions of others. Whether you're doing or delegating, remaining actively engaged helps ensure more of the positive aspects present themselves than the negative.

Being actively engaged doesn't mean you have to do it all. Even if you could, you would not want to. But you shouldn't delegate it all, either. Your influence should not be relegated to the reading experts in your school. There will always be somebody more qualified to lead reading-related initiatives than you are. Leadership isn't a contest and readers benefit when *everyone* takes an active posture towards literacy leadership.

The more active posture you take towards literacy leadership, the more nimble you will become. You may find yourself in a classroom modeling (a.k.a. doing) one minute, and then in a meeting where the most important thing you can do is to listen, learn, or invite others to lead (a.k.a. delegating). To illustrate the difference between a more active posture and being detached, I've added a Y Axis to the Literacy Leadership Continuum (see figure 6.3).

> Leadership isn't a contest and readers benefit when everyone takes an active posture towards literacy leadership.

The impact words (a.k.a. verbs) listed above the original delegating-doing continuum reflect some of the positive aspects of literacy

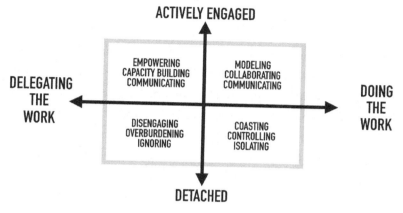

LITERACY LEADERSHIP POSTURE

ACTIVELY ENGAGED

DELEGATING THE WORK

EMPOWERING
CAPACITY BUILDING
COMMUNICATING

MODELING
COLLABORATING
COMMUNICATING

DOING THE WORK

DISENGAGING
OVERBURDENING
IGNORING

COASTING
CONTROLLING
ISOLATING

DETACHED

FROM "THE 6 LITERACY LEVERS" BY BRAD GUSTAFSON (2021)

Figure 6.3: **Literacy Leadership Posture**

leadership. The top two quadrants show how people may experience your leadership when you show up with a more active posture.

The bottom two quadrants show just the opposite. Just like before, you can probably think of quite a few additional words that could be placed in the quadrants. In fact, some words could even show up in more than one quadrant. The key is trying to show up actively, morally, and emotionally engaged as a literacy leader. And having the self-awareness to recognize when the posture and approach you're showing up with isn't getting the results you want or working for others.

I recognize all situations are different. The people and teams you interact with can be complicated. Sometimes your own mental health and ability to thrive will require you to temporarily detach from a person or situation. Or cause you to put up important boundaries on the work you're doing with others. I understand this and it connects back to you being the lever. The discernment, judgment, and posture you show up with matters.

The Levers in Action

This activity will help you show up to different literacy leadership situations with a more active posture. You'll put each of the levers into action using a scenario or practice you select. Before you do, I'm going to share how this works using a mundane example from my school. (You'll be selecting your own unique example in a second.)

Several years ago, we installed a few floating shelves in the staff lounge and started inviting teachers to let us know about books they'd like the school to invest in (see figure 6.4). We wanted to support teachers by making professional literature more accessible. But we also wanted to support informal conversations about professional learning, reading, and writing at the same time. And if I'm being completely honest, sprucing up the lounge so it felt more inspiring for our incredible teachers was also a goal.

The Staff Lounge Library has worked fairly well, and if you reflect on our purpose and approach you might even be able to identify a few levers involved in getting it up and running. However, the point of this activity isn't to look backward. It's to look at a current practice and apply each of the levers to it in order to see what's possible.

Here's how I envision putting the levers into action. Take an existing idea, practice, or scenario and consider what it could become if one of the levers were applied to it. For example, imagine what the Staff Lounge Library could become if we were more intentional with the invitations we extend? I could see us inviting 1-2 teachers a month to recommend books that showcase their strengths, interests, and aspirations for students.

To make the practice more relational and build community, we could invite the 1-2 featured teachers who recommended books to also

Figure 6.4: **Staff Lounge Library**

share a photo and short bio about their professional passions, family, or other interests. Adding this element could catapult the experience into something that connects our team on a different level.

Of course, you could take an entirely different approach and invite students to manage one of the floating shelves. Students could recommend and curate the books their classmates are buzzing about and add short booktalk blurbs or messages to their teachers. There are countless combinations of levers that could—and should—be applied to current practice.

1. Start by identifying a literacy practice or scenario you want to take a deeper look at. Write the name of the practice down in the middle box (see figure 6.5).

2. Next, think about the practice while applying different levers to it. Write down some of your thoughts and questions in the box that corresponds to the lever you're thinking about. You don't need to go in order and you can complete as many or as few of the boxes as you like.

3. Try to apply different combinations of levers to the practice you selected. Take notes about how the practice evolves based on the different ways you look at it as well as the questions you ask.

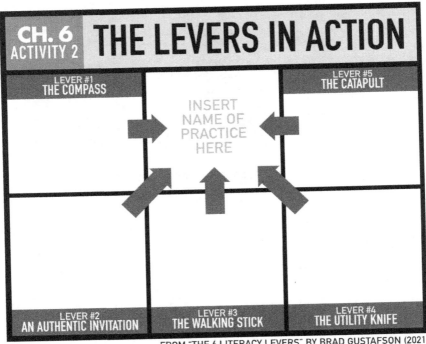

Figure 6.5: **The Levers in Action (Activity)**

4. Then, take action! Collaborate with colleagues and the readers you serve to push the field forward. Literacy leadership is a verb which brings us full circle to where you and I started this journey together.

Redefine Your Leadership

Earlier in the book I shared a definition for literacy leadership. That definition was built on the belief that choosing an active posture towards literacy is needed to impact lives and push the field forward.

This activity will help you redefine your leadership. It takes the definition I previously shared in chapter 1 and gives you a chance to make it your own.

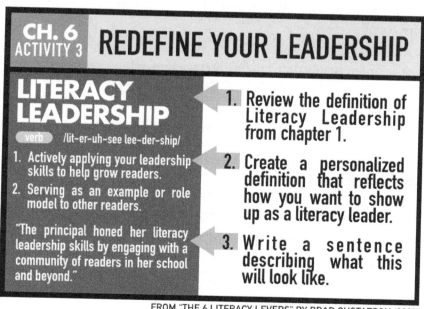

FROM "THE 6 LITERACY LEVERS" BY BRAD GUSTAFSON (2021)

Figure 6.6: **Redefine Your Leadership (Activity)**

1. Start by reviewing the definition above (originally found in chapter 1). Notice the active verbs and impact words within the definition and sample sentence.

2. Create a personalized definition for your literacy leadership. Be sure your definition includes how you want to show up as well as steps you will take right away. Write your definition down and put it somewhere you will see it often.

3. After writing your definition, add a sentence that shows what your literacy leadership will look like. I encourage you to think about an idea or commitment you can act upon right away and try to incorporate that into your sentence.

Unless you share the definition you composed on #LiteracyLever, there's very little chance our community of readers will know what you wrote. However, without even knowing what you wrote, I'm reasonably sure about a few things:

+ You probably didn't define literacy leadership as a flashy fix.
+ You probably want to lead meaningful change.
+ You probably want to lead on behalf of all readers.
+ And you definitely didn't talk about pine trees.

The 4th Pine Tree

The land we built our family cabin on was decimated by a tornado more than a decade ago. Part of the property that was once filled with old-growth pine trees is mostly weeds now. We wanted to reestablish the pine trees that once covered the land, so my youngest daughter and I transplanted several saplings from a nearby ditch. This was a learning experience for both of us.

The first pine tree we tried to transplant was a decent size sapling. That's what drew us to it in the first place. I imagined it would need less care than the smaller saplings that dotted the rest of the ditch. Unfortunately, the size of that first tree meant we needed to dig up more of the soil and root system around it, which also meant it was incredibly heavy and hard to move. It didn't take us long to realize we needed to start smaller.

The second pine tree we dug up took little effort to transplant. We handled it with care and threw a little water on it each day. Things started out okay, but that second tree struggled in the hottest summer months. Our motivation to water it evaporated as the needles turned yellowish-brown.

The third tree was different. We researched pine-tree transplanting techniques and learned that roots grow deepest when they are watered slowly, for longer periods of time. My daughter and I drilled a tiny hole in a five-gallon pail and filled the pail with water several times a week. This watering system allowed a consistent drip to seep deep into the soil and the roots of the tree followed. We went on to transplant several other saplings using the same deep-watering system and they're all thriving now. But there's a fourth pine tree I need to tell you about.

We noticed the fourth pine tree growing in the same area where we were bringing all the new transplants to. It didn't look like much at the time, but we decided to care for that fourth pine tree just like the newly planted trees. We added a watering system, mulch, and some decorative river rocks along the edge. It felt weird doing this to a tree that was already growing naturally in the wild. But something told me that the pre-established root system in the fourth pine tree might give it some sort of advantage over the trees we were transplanting. Fast forward to today, and the fourth tree is the tallest, greenest, and healthiest of them all. And to think we almost ignored it when we started the project.

I share this story for a couple reasons. It turns out there's a lot of science involved in growing trees. You can't skip over the soil work. There's value in starting small. Roots grow where the water goes. And the time to plant a tree is today.

But the fourth pine tree teaches another lesson. There are people you work with who have been doing lots of things right for a long period of time. Too often, initiatives are presented as *new* and everyone is made to feel as though their past work was wrong or no longer needed. If I learned anything from the fourth pine tree, it's that acknowledging the strengths and positive things already growing makes a big difference. Overlooking the talent and positive practices that have already taken root would be a detriment to what you're trying to grow together.

Including the people who have championed readers for a really long time in your next steps is a no brainer. But before you try to invite them into what you're wanting to change or grow, look for the things they've already established. Maybe you're needing to accept an invitation they've been silently sharing for some time. This doesn't mean you can't talk about new possibilities or that you should ignore practices that are problematic. I'm just saying that, too often, we ignore the contributions of people who are already leading.

Ideas You Can Implement

In the final pages we have together, I provide you with some additional tools, resources, and support to help you and your team take action today. Many of the resources from this book are also available on my website (BradGustafson.com). You'll also find some bonus content on the website to support your work with implementation. The resources in this chapter were designed to help you see and celebrate the incredible efforts and work being done around you. But they'll also help you push the field forward.

I organized them into a few different pathways for you to choose from. Each pathway includes a series of small steps you can choose to take. However, you can also pick and choose from the different ideas found in all three of the pathways to forge your own trail.

Path 1

The first path was designed to help you move from reflection to action. The path features a Literacy Lever Rubric that is divided into three sections; self, team, and school (see figure 6.7). This will allow you to use the rubric independently, with your team, or as a school.

To use the rubric, start by reading each statement and reflecting on the frequency in which you engage in an action. Before you decide on

LITERACY LEVER RUBRIC

			NOT YET	SOMETIMES	OFTEN
SELF	1	I collaborate with the readers I serve to create/update guiding beliefs.			
	2	I actively engage with a community of readers outside of school.			
	3	I am part of conversations that push the field forward.			
	4	I share my reading life with others in a variety of ways.			
	5	I create an environment where reading and relationships are celebrated.			
TEAM	1	We talk with students and each other about barriers to reading for fun.			
	2	We invite other teams and departments to collaborate on literacy work.			
	3	My team takes time to question individual and shared practices.			
	4	We empower all students to choose how they share their reading lives.			
	5	We plan experiences to connect around reading throughout the year.			
SCHOOL	1	Our school has a shared vision for literacy that actively informs decisions.			
	2	Our school's literacy work involves every educator and department.			
	3	Our school is using shared/common questions to champion readers.			
	4	Our school makes booktalks part of its core work and culture.			
	5	Our school is committed to daily independent reading time for all students.			

1 THE COMPASS	2 AN AUTHENTIC INVITATION	3 THE WALKING STICK	4 THE UTILITY KNIFE	5 THE CATAPULT

FROM "THE 6 LITERACY LEVERS" BY BRAD GUSTAFSON (2021)

Figure 6.7: **Literacy Lever Rubric**

the frequency, jot down examples or evidence of your engagement for each statement. Then, mark an "X" in the column that best describes your choice (i.e., Not Yet, Sometimes, or Often).

If you're completing the rubric with a team or as a school, talk about each statement and discuss the different examples you all bring to the work. If only one person has engaged with the action in a statement, they could reflect this in the "Self" section. However, the team should select the rubric column that reflects their collective commitment to a practice and the shared frequency a statement is demonstrated. The value in this activity comes from discussing the examples and experiences with your team and school. Oftentimes, we're not even aware of the best work being done by colleagues.

After you've completed the rubric (independently or with a team) take time to notice your individual strengths as well as the areas in which your team and school could benefit from additional focus. To support this follow-up, the statements within each section are aligned to different literacy levers. This will help you and your team circle back to specific chapters for ideas in the areas you're needing to focus on.

Determine a date you will revisit the rubric and examples you and your team wrote down. If you completed the rubric with a team or school staff, I'd also suggest checking in informally on a more regular basis to keep the conversation going. These check-ins could be quick words of encouragement, sharing something you noticed, or involve more in-depth discussion at a Professional Learning Community (PLC) meeting.

Path 2

The second path will help you plan and facilitate your first five monthly meetings of the year. Of course, you could adapt the frequency and format to fit department or PLC meetings as well. The goal is to help you get started and build momentum. The overarching goal of this path is to engage your staff in an ongoing and collective effort to support each and every reader—just like watering a pine tree!

Each meeting builds upon the previous meeting in a small but meaningful way. This path was also designed to be accessible to everyone on staff; it is not reserved for only the select few who may have formal literacy roles. Each of the five meetings is designed to last between 30-45 minutes and includes:

+ A learning focus
+ A picture book recommendation to support the learning focus
+ Discussion questions to initiate conversation
+ A call-to-action to create community and activate change

The first monthly meeting agenda is mocked up below (see figure 6.8). The theme for the first meeting is *Creating a Compass*, and it aligns with the first chapter of *The 6 Literacy Levers*. The read-aloud book I'm recommending was strategically selected to support the theme. You know your school and colleagues better than anyone, so feel free to adjust the activities and pacing as you see fit.

As you read through the first meeting agenda, I'm sure you'll notice things you'd structure differently or things you'd like to add. For example, I structured the first call-to-action as an activity everyone engages with in a small group format. However, when we worked through this meeting as a school, I introduced the activity to the entire group, although most of the in-depth conversations occurred in follow-up meetings with PLCs. We actually spent a couple of months on this step. From there, a schoolwide compass that reflects the beliefs, research, and rights we want all readers to have was developed.

You could choose to modify any of the call-to-action sections by pulling from the schoolwide implementation challenges found at the end of each chapter. To help you customize each meeting, I'm including a blank template (see figure 6.9).

PLANNING YOUR FIRST FIVE
MONTHLY MEETINGS
#1: CREATING THE COMPASS

LEARNING FOCUS
▸ PARTICIPANTS WILL CO-CREATE GUIDING LITERACY BELIEFS

READ ALOUD
▸ READ "WHAT THE ROAD SAID" BY CLEO WADE WITH ILLUSTRATIONS BY LUCIE DE MOYENCOURT

DISCUSSION QUESTIONS
1. WHERE DO WE WANT TO LEAD THE READERS WE SERVE?
2. WHAT DO WE HOPE TO SEE ALONG THE WAY?
3. HOW WILL WE KNOW WHEN WE GET THERE?

CALL-TO-ACTION
▸ INVITE SMALL GROUPS TO JOT DOWN WORDS AND BELIEFS ABOUT READING ONTO STICKY NOTES AND CHART PAPER
▸ NEXT, ASK THEM TO ORGANIZE THEIR STICKY NOTES BY THEME
▸ THEN, HAVE SMALL GROUPS DO A GALLERY WALK TO INTERACT WITH THE STICKY NOTES OTHER GROUPS CREATED
▸ AFTER THAT, CHALLENGE EACH GROUP TO CREATE A VISUAL (E.G., COMPASS, CORE BELIEFS, OTHER ANALOGY) REFLECTING WHAT THEY WANT EVERY READER TO EXPERIENCE

FROM "THE 6 LITERACY LEVERS" BY BRAD GUSTAFSON (2021)

Figure 6.8: **Monthly Meeting Agenda #1**

Content for meetings 2-5 is below. I encourage you to use the template to plug in whatever content meets the needs of your team. The important step is starting. The best time to plant a tree is not next week or next year, but right now.

Monthly Meeting #2: An Authentic Invitation
   Learning Focus: Participants will discuss how to create a reading community in which everyone feels a sense of belonging.
   Read Aloud: *Our Table* by Peter H. Reynolds

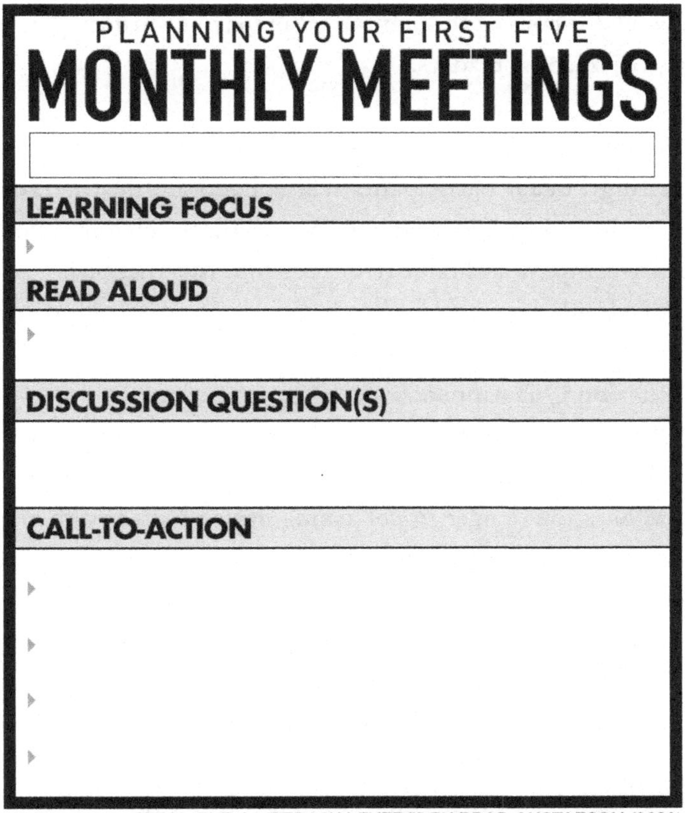

FROM "THE 6 LITERACY LEVERS" BY BRAD GUSTAFSON (2021)

Figure 6.9: **Monthly Meeting Template**

Discussion Questions:

1. In what ways might the compass you created at the last meeting connect to the table being built in this story?
2. What is our "literacy table" in this school and how will we ensure everyone experiences a strong sense of belonging?

Call-to-Action:

+ Invite a colleague (or group of colleagues) to take action. Work together to make your school's reading community more inclusive. Wondering where to start? Look for spaces and places where it feels as though the table may be shrinking or inaccessible to some readers.

Monthly Meeting #3: Choosing a Walking Stick

Learning Focus: Participants will collaborate on the creation of 2-3 guiding questions that support deeper implementation of the literacy compass and table (from the first two meetings).

Read Aloud: *Just Ask!* by Sonia Sotomayor with illustrations by Rafael López.

Discussion Questions:

1. In what ways does the story reflect our previous conversations about building a literacy table where everyone belongs?

2. What's the danger in *not* asking important (or difficult) questions about our practices and the impact they have on readers?

Call-to-Action:

* Work together to create 2-3 questions that could be asked in different meetings or decision-points over the course of the year. The questions should reflect the beliefs and conversations you had about the literacy compass and table. For example, if your literacy compass shows that *reading identity is important*, you might write down a question like, "*How does this decision, book, or practice show students we value their reading identities?*"

Monthly Meeting #4: They All Saw a Utility Knife

Learning Focus: Participants will practice talking about books in a manner that's meaningful to them.

Recommended Read Aloud: *They All Saw a Cat* by Brendan Wenzel

Discussion Questions:

1. Which animal's perspective surprised you? Did any of their perspectives resonate?

2. When you look at the utility knife (i.e., a booktalk), what do you see?

Call-to-Action:

- Invite everyone to think about the first book or chapter book they remember reading or enjoying. After giving everyone a chance to share in small groups, challenge them to share a booktalk with a student, colleague, or family before the next meeting.

Monthly Meeting #5: The Transformative Power of the Catapult

Learning Focus: Participants will discuss the ways their school supports relationships, connection, and community.

Recommended Read Aloud: *Blue Floats Away* by Travis Jonker with illustrations by Grant Snider

Discussion Questions:

1. What are the things that might make readers want to float away from school?
2. In thinking about how Blue transformed and came back as part of the water cycle, what aspects of our reading community might lead to transformation, renewal, and reconnecting?

Call-to-Action:

- Start by inviting participants to discuss the role of relationships and connection in each of the first four meeting themes (i.e., Creating the Compass, An Authentic Invitation, Choosing a Walking Stick, and They All Saw a Utility Knife). Then, work together to identify an area of practice or school event that could be made even more relational and connected for readers.

I want to highlight two important pieces before moving on to the third path. First, the prominent role that picture books play in each of the meetings is intentional. The picture books I'm recommending support the theme and learning focus for each meeting, but they model how picture books can support learning and conversation for all ages. Of course, if you come across books that better support a theme or your team's needs, feel free to switch out what I suggested.

I also want to encourage you to be on the lookout for ways to create additional connection between meetings. The conversations and learning that occurs between formal meeting times is an invaluable part of the work.

Path 3

The third path was designed to help you initiate conversations and create connection with and between other literacy leaders, whether they are in a classroom down the hallway, in a neighboring school, or halfway around the world. The path features all the resources you need to organize an engaging book study. Some of the components can even be incorporated into a university class. The menu below provides an overview of the resource options (see figure 6.10).

Character-Based Questions:

[**Introduction**] The story starts out with a challenging meeting. Where do you like to go to reflect and recharge after difficult days?

[**Chapter 1**] Dayo and the young woman in the café have a joy-filled conversation connected to reading. What do you wonder about this? What does this remind you of?

[**Chapter 2**] The invitation Dayo reads aloud in the café says, "Who will you choose?" If you could meet a favorite author or reading champion for dinner, who would it be and why?

[**Chapter 3**] The conversation you have with your mystery-reading mentor is genuine and effortless. What helps you to have conversations that feel safe and authentic?

THE 6 LITERACY LEVERS
BOOK STUDY MENU

CHARACTER-BASED QUESTIONS
QUESTIONS TO HELP YOU CONNECT WITH CHARACTERS FROM THE
BOOK AND EACH OTHER

SOCIAL-MEDIA SAVVY QUESTIONS
EXTRA-SHARABLE DISCUSSION STARTERS FOR ONLINE
ENVIRONMENTS

QUESTIONS TO PUSH THE FIELD
A COLLECTION OF BRAD'S FAVORITE QUESTIONS FROM THE BOOK

IDEA EXCHANGE
PROMPTS TO SUPPORT COLLABORATION AND IDEA SHARING

NOTABLE & QUOTABLE
QUESTIONS TO HELP YOU DISCUSS SOME OF THE QUOTES AND
POWERFUL LANGUAGE FOUND IN THE BOOK

BONUS VIDEO CONTENT
MORE AUTHENTIC INSIGHTS FROM BRAD AT BRADGUSTAFSON.COM

**MIX AND MATCH TO MEET THE NEEDS OF YOUR
BOOK STUDY, UNIVERSITY CLASS, OR SCHOOL**

FROM "THE 6 LITERACY LEVERS" BY BRAD GUSTAFSON (2021)

Figure 6.10: **Book Study Menu**

[**Chapter 4**] In this chapter, Lydia is wearing a shirt that says, "I SLAY READING LOGS." What is a practice you'd like to slay on behalf of the readers you serve?

[**Chapter 5**] Dayo and Lydia invite you into a book club in this chapter. If you were to recommend two books for them to consider reading in the book club, what would they be and why?!

201

[**Chapter 6**] At the end of the story Dayo asks, "So what should *we* do now?" How would you respond to him?

Social-Media Savvy Questions:

[**Introduction**] Students who are successful readers have the capacity to be more successful in nearly every other academic area (Irvin et al., 2010). How are you helping students succeed? #LiteracyLever

[**Chapter 1**] Share a selfie with a book you're reading! #LiteracyLever

[**Chapter 1**] What's a leadership quote that inspires you? (Bonus points for sharing in meme form.) #LiteracyLever

[**Chapter 2**] If you were to invite us into a literacy project or passion project you're working on, what would you say? #LiteracyLever

[**Chapter 2**] What does your reading flow zone look like? #LiteracyLever

[**Chapter 3**] What's your favorite question to ask readers? #LiteracyLever

[**Chapter 3**] Can you share a time when you felt you had Shiny Book Report Syndrome (S.B.R.S)? #LiteracyLever

[**Chapter 4**] What was the first chapter book or series you remember reading? #LiteracyLever

[**Chapter 4**] Tell us about a book you're reading (or recently finished) using emojis. #LiteracyLever

[**Chapter 5**] Give a shout out to the literacy leaders in your life. Who are the people who challenge and inspire you? #LiteracyLever

[**Chapter 5**] If you were to create a baseball card for yourself, what are some surprising stats and fun facts you'd add to the back? #LiteracyLever

[**Chapter 6**] Share a photo or GIF of what it looks like when you're owning your role as a literacy lever. Be sure to use our community hashtag when posting. #LiteracyLever

[Chapter 6] What's one way you will take a more active posture when it comes to literacy leadership? #LiteracyLever

Questions to Push the Field:

[Chapter 1] What would you say your literacy "true north" is?

[Chapter 2] What are some things you can do right now to help students and colleagues find their reading flow?

[Chapter 3] What would school look like if we carried a walking stick that helped us confront potentially damaging practices with curiosity and questions?

[Chapter 4] How will you keep booktalks authentic and not turn them into yet another assignment or "string" a school ties to the reading lives of students?

[Chapter 5] What processes, procedures, or systems need to be updated to ensure every reader feels seen and supported within your reading community?

[Chapter 6] What would you do next if you decided to fully embrace the fact that *you* are an important lever in the lives of readers?

Idea Exchange:

[Chapter 1] Share something you'd suggest to any team or school that might be trying to create a common literacy compass.

[Chapter 2] What are some of the most meaningful literacy experiences you've been invited into (as a student or literacy leader)?

[Chapter 3] Share one way you've tried to strengthen students' long-term relationship with reading?

[Chapter 4] What are some other ideas to integrate booktalks into the culture of a classroom or school?

[Chapter 5] Share one idea you have to build relationships, create connection, or strengthen the reading community in your school.

[**Chapter 6**] Share an idea you've tried that's helped you take a more active posture in your literacy leadership.

Notable & Quotable:

[**Introduction**] "Somebody is looking to you to lead right now." Who does this quote from Richard DuFour and Robert Marzano make you think of?

[**Chapter 1**] "Being willing to do what you are not qualified to do is sometimes what qualifies you." Based on this quote from Bill Johnson, what is one thing you feel unqualified to do that you're willing to do?

[**Chapter 2**] "Sometimes the greatest gift you can give another person is to simply include them." How do you know when you belong? What might be missing when you don't feel a strong sense of belonging?

[**Chapter 3**] "You can't teach what you don't know. You can't lead where you won't go." In thinking about this quote from Gary Howard, are there places that are harder for you to go or questions that are more difficult for you to ask? Why?

[**Chapter 4**] "Booktalks are like kryptonite to people who say they aren't readers yet!" When was the last time you told somebody about a book? How intentional are you about sharing books you love with students who may not see themselves as readers yet?

[**Chapter 5**] "Connection is the energy that is created between people when they feel seen, heard, and valued—when they can give and receive without judgement." Brené Brown shares this beautiful quote about connection. How would you describe connection when it comes to readers and books?

[**Chapter 6**] "My courage gives you permission to be courageous." What does this quote from Anthony Muhammed make you think about?

[**All**] What other language or quotes from the book stuck out to you? Why?

Unfinished Business

> Because helping all kids *learn* to read while ensuring they also *want* to read is a priceless pursuit worthy of your leadership.

If you commit to creating a collage that serves every reader there is no telling what your school's culture of literacy will look like one, two, or three years from now. But this is also the time to start. My hope for you, now, is that you trust yourself. Humbly acknowledge there is much to learn and that there always will be. Then, apply the levers with all your heart. Because helping all kids learn to read while ensuring they also *want* to read is a priceless pursuit worthy of your leadership.

> *"What does it matter if a child can read better but chooses to never read again due to their hatred of the tools we used to get them there?"*
> ~Pernille Ripp

Questions to Push the Field Forward

+ What is one thing you'll do tomorrow to make a difference in the lives of the readers you serve?
+ Who in your sphere of influence is not part of the collage yet? How will you invite, invest in, and include them?

Leverage Your Literacy Leadership Schoolwide

You are an important literacy lever in your classroom, school, or district. You can help activate all the other levers. In doing so, you will help create a literacy collage capable of supporting readers into their future.

Challenge yourself to look for opportunities to apply the levers in different ways. Then, work with your colleagues to identify a schoolwide topic or practice to look at collectively. This is an opportunity for everyone to bring their strengths and curiosity to the table. Work together to transform the practice until it supports each reader you serve.

Learning to read is one of the most important things a student will ever do in your school. Each of us needs to take an active role in creating the culture and conditions that ensure all students learn how to read *and* that they want to read. This is not a responsibility that should be relegated to specific roles, levels, or departments within your school.

Your influence—your leadership—is an invaluable part of the collage. Your resolve to carry the compass, accept and extend invitations, ask questions, lead booktalks, create connection, and foster meaningful

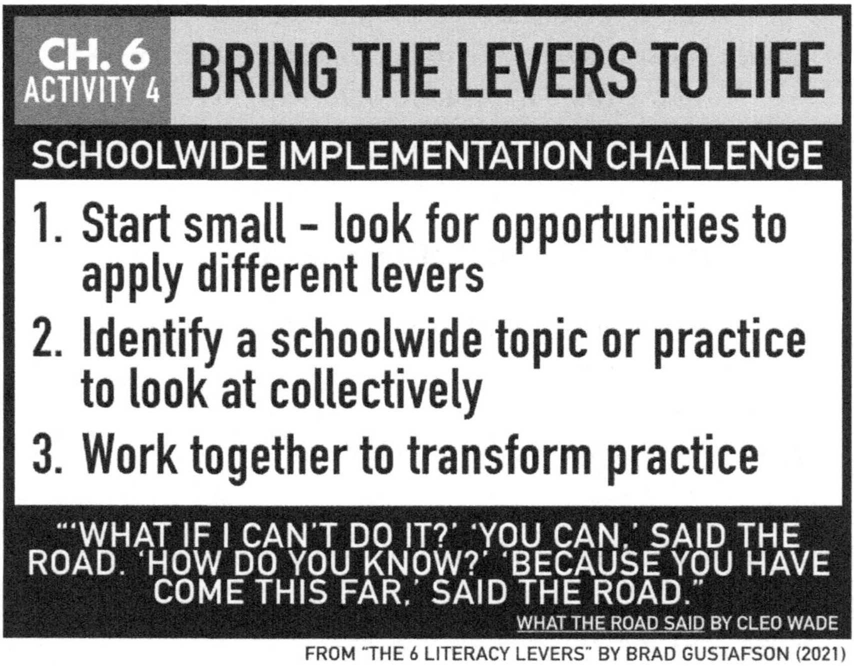

CH. 6 ACTIVITY 4 BRING THE LEVERS TO LIFE

SCHOOLWIDE IMPLEMENTATION CHALLENGE

1. **Start small – look for opportunities to apply different levers**
2. **Identify a schoolwide topic or practice to look at collectively**
3. **Work together to transform practice**

"'WHAT IF I CAN'T DO IT?' 'YOU CAN,' SAID THE ROAD. 'HOW DO YOU KNOW?' 'BECAUSE YOU HAVE COME THIS FAR,' SAID THE ROAD."
WHAT THE ROAD SAID BY CLEO WADE

FROM "THE 6 LITERACY LEVERS" BY BRAD GUSTAFSON (2021)

Figure 6.11: **Schoolwide Implementation Challenge**

relationships will directly impact the results you and your team achieve. This thing you're building matters and it will enhance every other priority at your school.

The Story Continues

Imagine this: Laughter and questions reverberate throughout the café. Before Dayo officially begins your book club meeting, you pause to take it all in. How the space feels. The energy. The books and connection. Your eyes drift down to the compass design set into the surface of the floor. You can still picture the spot where the boy left his marshmallowy book for you.

As more feet shuffle in and across the compass, you look up. Your heart skips a beat when you see a parent from your school. Not just any parent, but *that* parent. The sting from the meeting you had with them still smarts. Yet, somehow when they see you sitting in this circle, they smile. And it appears genuine.

The rollercoaster of emotions and accompanying questions you have are interrupted when Dayo clears his throat. He's holding the camera again. As Dayo invites everyone in the book club to come together for a picture, you look back at the parent. And offer a genuine smile in return. The collage is growing.

References

Allington, R. L., McGill-Franzen, A., Camilli, G., Williams, L., Graff, J., Zeig, J., Zmach, C., & Nowak, R. (2010). Addressing summer reading setback among economically disadvantaged elementary students. *Reading Psychology*, 31(5), 411–427.

Allington, R. & Gabriel, R. (2012). Every child, every day. *Educational Leadership*, Vol. 69, No. 6. March, pp. 10-15.

Allington, R. (2013). What really matters when working with struggling readers. *The Reading Teacher*, 66(7), 520-530.

Allington, R. (2014). How reading volume affects both reading fluency and reading achievement. *International Electronic Journal of Elementary Education*, 2014, 7(1), 13-26.

Anderson, A. & James, D. (2020). Leading change that lasts: A framework for forging change that Lasts. *District Management Journal*, 27 (Winter 2020), 16-35.

Anderson, R. C., Wilson P.T., Fielding, L.G. (1988). Growth in reading and how children spend their time outside of school. *Reading Research Quarterly*, No.23, pp. 285-303.

Bailey, L. B., Silvern, S. B., Brabham, E., & Ross, M. (2004). The effects of interactive reading homework and parent involvement on children's inference responses. *Early Childhood Education Journal*, 32(3), 173–178.

Baker, P. & Moss, R. K. (1993). Creating a community of readers. *School Community Journal*, 3(1), Spring/Summer.

Becker, M., McElvany, N., & Kortenbruck, M. (2010). Intrinsic and extrinsic reading motivation as predictors of reading literacy: A longitudinal study. *Journal of Educational Psychology*, 102(4), 773–785.

Bishop, R. S. (1990). Mirrors, windows, and sliding glass doors. *Perspectives: Choosing and Using Books for the Classroom*, 6(3), Summer.

Booth, D. W. & Rowsell, J. (2007). *The literacy principal: Leading, supporting, and assessing reading and writing initiatives*. Pembroke Publishers.

Brunow, V. (2016). Authentic literacy experiences in the secondary classroom. *Language and Literacy Spectrum*, 26, 60-74.

Daniels, E. & Steres, M. (2011). Examining the effects of a school-wide reading culture on the engagement of middle school students. *RMLE Online*, 35(2), 1–13.

Dietrich T. & Balli, S. J. (2014). Digital natives: Fifth-grade students' authentic and ritualistic engagement with technology. *International Journal of Instruction*, 7(2), 21-34.

Djikic, M., & Oatley, K. (2014). The art in fiction: From indirect communication to changes of the self. *Psychology of Aesthetics, Creativity, and the Arts*, 8(4), 498–505.

Dufour, R. & Marzano, R. (2011). *Leaders of learning: How district, school, and classroom leaders improve student achievement*. Solution Tree Press.

Edmonds, C. (2018). The leader's primary contribution: Discretionary energy. *Purposeful Culture Group*. Retrieved October 2, 2021, from https://www.drivingresultsthroughculture.com/2011/03/28/the-leaders-primary-contribution-discretionary-energy/.

Ferlazzo, L. (2019). Response: Reading logs should be tools for students to spy on themselves. *Education Week*, July 10, 2019.

Fisher, D. & Frey, N. (2018). Raise reading volume through access, choice, discussion, and book talks. *International Literacy Association*, 72(1), 89-97.

Flachbart, M. (2019). Helping students with dyslexia find their reading motivation. *Education Northwest*. Retrieved October 3, 2021, from https://.educationnorthwest.org/northwest-matters/helping-students-dyslexia-find-their-reading-motivation.

Gabriel, R. (2021). The sciences of reading instruction. *ASCD*. Retrieved October 3, 2021, from https://www.ascd.org/el/articles/the-sciences-of-reading-instruction.

Gillies, A. (2017). Teaching pre-service teachers about belonging. *International Journal of Whole Schooling*, Special Issue, 17-25.

Godin, S. (2020). *The practice: Shipping creative work*. Penguin Books.

Goodwin, B. (2020). *Research matters: Cracking the reading code*. ASCD.

Guthrie, J. T., Wigfield, A., Humenick, N. M., Perencevich, K. C., Taboada, A., & Barbosa, P. (2006). Influences of stimulating tasks on reading motivation and comprehension. *The Journal of Educational Research*, 99(4), 232–246.

Hall, L. A. (2014). How reading identities are formed [video]. YouTube. https://www.youtube.com/watch?v=nuYhh6lVsXw

Harvey, S. & Ward, A. (2017). *From striving to thriving: How to grow confident, capable readers*. New York: Scholastic Teaching Resources.

Havran, M. (2019). Teaching the reading life: Making the invisible visible. *Texas Journal of Literacy Education*, 7(2), 13-21.

Hiebert, E. H., & Reutzel, D. R. (2010), *Revisiting silent reading: New directions for teachers and researchers*. Newark, DE: International Reading Association.

Houck, B. D., & Novak, S. (2016). *Literacy unleashed: Fostering excellent reading instruction through classroom visits*. ASCD.

International Literacy Association (2018). The power and promise of read-alouds and independent reading, Retrieved October 10, 2021, from https://www.literacyworldwide.org/docs/default-source/where-we-stand/ila-power-promise-read-alouds-in-dependent-reading.pdf.

International Dyslexia Association (2018). Knowledge and practice standards for teachers of reading, Retrieved October 21, 2021, from https://app.box.com/s/21gdk2k1p3bnagdfz1xy0v98j5ytl1wk.

Irvin, J. L. (2010). *Taking the lead on adolescent literacy: Action steps for schoolwide success*. Corwin Press.

REFERENCES

Jacobson, L. (2017). Building a culture of literacy: Ideas for making literacy the foundation in your school. *Literacy Today*, 20–24.

Kittle, P. (2020). Let them read, please. *Educational Leadership*, 77(5), 77-81.

Krashen, S. (2004). *The power of reading: Insights from the research.* Westport, CT: Libraries Unlimited.

Kruger, J. & Dunning, D. (1999). Unskilled and unaware of it: How difficulties in recognizing one's own incompetence lead to inflated self-assessments. *Journal of Personality and Social Psychology*, 77(6), 1121–1134.

Kuşdemir, Y. & Bulut, P. (2018). The relationship between elementary school students' reading comprehension and reading motivation. *Journal of Education and Training Studies*, 6(12), 97.

Lindsay, J. (2010). *Children's access to print material and education-related outcomes: Findings from a meta-analytic review.* Learning Point Associates.

Locher, F. M., Becker, S. & Pfost, M. (2019). The relation between students' intrinsic reading motivation and book reading in recreational and school contexts. *AERA Open*, 5(2), 233285841985204.

Marinak, B. A. & Gambrell, L. B. (2016). *No more reading for junk: Best practices for motivating readers.* Heinemann.

McCullough, L. (2020). Barriers and assistance for female leaders in academic STEM in the US. *Education Sciences*, 10(10), 264.

McClung, N. A., Barry, E., Neebe, D., Mere-Cook, Y, Wang, Q., Gonzalez-Balsam, M. (2019). Choice matters: Equity and literacy achievement. *Berkeley Review of Education*, 8(2), 147-178.

Meltzer, E. & Arnold, J. (2020). How love became a weapon in the reading wars. *Breaking The Code.* Retrieved October 3, 2021, from https://www.breakingthecode.com/how-love-became-a-weapon-in-the-reading-wars/.

Mercer, D. K. (2016). Who is the building leader? Commentary on educational leadership preparation programs for the future. *Educational Considerations*, 43(4).

Michels, D. & Murphy, K. (2021, August 31). How good is your company at change? *Harvard Business Review.* Retrieved October 2, 2021, from https://hbr.org/2021/07/how-good-is-your-company-at-change.

Miller, D., Kelley, S. & Lesesne, T. S. (2014). *Reading in the wild: The book whisperer's keys to cultivating lifelong reading habits.* Jossey-Bass.

Miller, D. & Moss, B. (2013). *No more independent reading without support.* Portsmouth, NH: Heinemann.

NASSP (2005). Creating a culture of literacy: A guide for middle and high school principals. Retrieved October 2, 2021, from https://www.nassp.org/wp-content/uploads/2020/05/Creating-a-Culture-of-Literacy-Guide.pdf.

National Council of Teachers of English (2019). Position statement on independent reading. *NCTE*, Position Retrieved October 10, 2021, from https://ncte.org/statement/independent-reading/.

Pak, S. & Weseley, A. J. (2012). The effect of mandatory reading logs on children's motivation to read. *Journal of Research in Education*, 22(1), 251-265.

Pink, D. (2009). *Drive: The surprising truth about what motivates us.* Riverhead Books.

Raza, S. A. & Sikandar, A. (2018). Impact of leadership style of teacher on the performance of students: An application of Herset and Blanchard situational model. *Bulletin of Education and Research*, 40(3) 73-94.

Ripp, P. (2/13/21). If you see no value in the books in your library, why should students? If you say you have no… [Tweet], Twitter, https://twitter.com/pernilleripp/status/1360591931265454083?s=20.

Ripp, P. (5/26/21). So much of what we do comes down to kids feeling good on their reading journey, no matter where… [Tweet], Twitter, https://twitter.com/pernilleripp/status/1397525380752367620?s=20.

Rodrigo, V., Greenberg, D., Burke, V., Hall, R., Berry, A., Brinck, T., Joseph, H., Oby, M. (2007). Implementing an extensive reading program and library for adult literacy learners. *Reading in a Foreign Language*, 19(2), 106-119.

Scoggin, J. & Schneewind, H. (n.d.). Reading identity and why it matters. Retrieved October 3, 2021, from https://blog.heinemann.com/reading-identity-and-why-it-matters-by-jennifer-scoggin-and-hannah-schneewind.

Shepherd, A. C. & Taylor, R. T. (2019). An analysis of factors which Influence high school administrators' readiness and confidence to provide digital instructional leadership. *International Journal of Educational Leadership Preparation*, 14(1), 52-76.

Simonton, D. K. (1988). *Scientific genius*. New York: Cambridge University Press.

Sinek, S. (2019). *Start with why: How great leaders inspire everyone to take action*. Penguin Business.

Staloch, T. (2002). *A case study on the relationship between restitution and the transformational leadership behaviors of selected school principals*. ProQuest Dissertations Publishing.

Sullivan, A. & Brown, M. (2013). Social Inequalities in cognitive scores at age 16: The role of reading. London: Centre for Longitudinal Studies.

Sullivan, A., & Brown, M. (2015). Reading for pleasure and progress in vocabulary and mathematics. *British Educational Research Journal*, 41(6), 971–991.

Waedaoh, A. & Sinwongsuwat, K. (2018). Enhance English language learners' conversation abilities via CA-informed sitcom lessons. *Canadian Center of Science and Education*, 11(12), 121-130.

Wahlstrom, K. L., Louis, K. S., Leithwood, K. A., & Anderson, S. E. (2010). *Learning from leadership: Investigating the links to improved student learning*. Educational Research Service.

Wallace Foundation (2013). Five key responsibilities - the school principal as leader: Guiding schools to better teaching and learning. Wallace Foundation. Retrieved October 2, 2021, from https://www.wallacefoundation.org/knowledge-center/pages/key-responsibilities-the-school-principal-as-leader.aspx.

Whittingham, J. & Rickman, W. A. (2015). Booktalking: Avoiding summer drift. *American Association of School Librarians*, 43(5), 18-21.

Wigfield, A., Gladstone, J. R. & Turci, L. (2016). Beyond cognition: Reading motivation and reading comprehension. *Child Development Perspectives*, 10(3), 190–195.

About the Author

Dr. Brad Gustafson is an award-winning principal, best-selling author, speaker, and avid reader. He understands the critical role leaders play in creating the conditions where students *want* to read...even after it's no longer required of them.

Brad co-hosts a weekly webcast called *Read This Now* where he talks about literacy and shares book recommendations with fellow literacy leaders. He has served on the Scholastic Principal Advisory Board and been a national advisor with Future Ready Schools for several years.

Brad was also named Minnesota's Principal of the Year in 2016, and a National School Boards Association "20 to Watch." His school has been recognized at the local, state, and national level. From classrooms to the boardroom (and beyond), Brad is helping educators own their influence as leaders of literacy.

Keynotes, Workshops, and Professional Learning

The 6 Literacy Levers

Leaders at every level of your organization (formal and informal) play an important role in growing readers. Learn how to apply key literacy levers to increase reading motivation, confront potentially problematic practices, and co-create a reading community. This interactive keynote is packed with actionable ideas and the practitioner-friendly research your team needs to take your next best steps forward together.

Reclaiming Our Calling

Imagine what school would look like if we all held the whole learner in the same regard as high-stakes test scores. Let's talk about how educators are tapping into their own strengths and making relationships a priority in school. This keynote is a refreshingly honest message that will help inspire you and your team to hold on to the heart, mind, and hope of the work we're called to do together.

Renegade Leadership

Creating innovative schools requires leadership and intentionality. This keynote, based on the best-selling book from Corwin Press, will change the way you think about innovation and technology leadership. Learn how to lead through pedagogy and unleash student and staff potential using the Renegade CODE. Meaningful change is within your reach, but it will require your leadership!

For additional information on workshops, consulting, and virtual-professional development, go to BradGustafson.com

Acknowledgements

Writing a book is a team effort. The MVP of our team is my wife, Deb. Without her sacrifice and support there would be no book.

The inspiring professionals I've served alongside in my school and district have been instrumental in my growth. Literacy leaders like Linda Gibbons, Julie Kirchner, Sharon Lapensky, Julie Schneider, Kim Connor, Sarabeth deNeui, Kate Ronning, and E. J. Smith have not only shown me the way, but they've helped me find my own way. The teachers and grade-level teams (some of whom were referenced in this book) have also helped me see what's possible when we start with the things readers need from us, and then chart a course together from there. And our school's incredible administrative professional, Kallie Spaulding, who provides leadership and support in helping us move from vision to tangible actions that support and inspire readers.

I also want to thank some of my friends and the people in my professional learning network who have contributed so much to my thinking and leadership. Donalyn Miller, Todd Nesloney, Liz Garden, John Schu, Dana Boyd, LaQuita Outlaw, Colby Sharp, Lynmara Colón, Eric Skanson, Julie Bloss, Steven Weber, and Steven Geis are a constant source of inspiration and learning. As are many more.

I want to thank the ConnectEDD Publishing team and family for their support. I've been blessed to have worked with several incredible people and publishers over the years, and Jimmy Casas and Jeff Zoul are among the best. Their steadfast support, coaching, professionalism, and passion helped us create a book we think will empower leaders for a long time.

And speaking of a loooong time...*The 6 Literacy Levers* has been more than five years in the making. While many people had a hand in how it took shape, the book would be a shell of itself without the feedback and perspective shared by Pernille Ripp. Words can't express the depth of appreciation I have for her commitment to pushing the field forward. Or her caring and courageous approach.

On a loosely-related note, the pages of this book were being crafted long before my second book, *Reclaiming Our Calling*, was published. If you've already read *Reclaiming Our Calling*, you may have noticed a love of literacy in its DNA as well. (If you haven't read the book yet, I hope you'll look for this if you ever have a chance to read it.) I suppose the undercurrents of literacy and magic that made Mrs. MacLean work were my attempt at inviting more educators into the work of raising readers.

Lastly, I want to thank Jennifer LaGarde for her friendship, feedback, and all the laughs we've shared over the years. Whether we're talking about books on our weekly webcast, arguing about who consumes more water over the course of a day, or collaborating on connected literacy projects...her genius is a gift I don't take for granted. As the saying goes, the well runs deep with Jenn, and I'm eternally grateful for her work.

More from
ConnectEDD Publishing

Since 2015, ConnectEDD has worked to transform education by empowering educators to become better-equipped to teach, learn, and lead. What started as a small company designed to provide professional learning events for educators has grown to include a variety of services to help teachers and administrators address essential challenges. ConnectEDD offers instructional and leadership coaching, professional development workshops focusing on a variety of educational topics, a roster of nationally recognized educator associates who possess hands-on knowledge and experience, educational conferences custom-designed to meet the specific needs of schools, districts, and state/national organizations, and ongoing, personalized support, both virtually and onsite. In 2020, ConnectEDD expanded to include publishing services designed to provide busy educators with books and resources consisting of practical information on a wide variety of teaching, learning, and leadership topics. Please visit us online at connecteddbooks.org or contact us at: info@connecteddpublishing.com

Recent Publications:

Live Your Excellence: Action Guide by Jimmy Casas

Culturize: Action Guide by Jimmy Casas

Daily Inspiration for Educators: Positive Thoughts for Every Day of the Year by Jimmy Casas

Eyes on Culture: Multiply Excellence in Your School by Emily Paschall

Pause. Breathe. Flourish. Living Your Best Life as an Educator by William D. Parker

L.E.A.R.N.E.R. Finding the True, Good, and Beautiful in Education by Marita Diffenbaugh

Educator Reflection Tips Volume II: Refining Our Practice by Jami Fowler-White

Handle With Care: Managing Difficult Situations in Schools with Dignity and Respect by Jimmy Casas and Joy Kelly

Disruptive Thinking: Preparing Learners for Their Future by Eric Sheninger

Permission to be Great: Increasing Engagement in Your School by Dan Butler

Be the Flame: Sparking Positive Classroom Communities by Shane Saeed

Daily Inspiration for Educators: Positive Thoughts for Every Day of the Year, Volume II by Jimmy Casas